THE LANGUAGE OF WINNERS!

By

World Champion
José Luis "Jay-el" Hinojosa, MD

Copyright © 2012 José Luis Hinojosa

All rights reserved.

ISBN: 0985729708

ISBN-13: 978-0-9857297-0-7

Also by José Luis "Jay-el" Hinojosa, MD

NOVELS

The Tonic

Master and Disciple

PLAYS

Exam Room 2

Rosi Milagros

NONFICTION

Report Card on Rape

Magnets for Health

Tae Kwon Do for Everyone

The HELP Secret

Frozen in Time

SCREENPLAYS

Campeón (co-author)

Contents –

Dedication		page 6
Acknowledgments		page 8
Foreword	by Presley Swagerty	page 10
Preamble		page 12
Alphabet		page 19
Chapter 1	Attitude	page 26
Chapter 2	Believe	page 36
Chapter 3	Call me!	page 44
Chapter 4	Discipline	page 53
Chapter 5	Education	page 61
Chapter 6	Focus	page 72
Chapter 7	Giving	page 81
Chapter 8	Habits	page 88
Chapter 9	Insults	page 95
Chapter 10	Just right!	page 107

Chapter 11	Kinetics	page 115
Chapter 12	Leadership	page 121
Chapter 13	Mannerisms	page 128
Chapter 14	Network	page 136
Chapter 15	Options	page 142
Chapter 16	Patience	page 150
Chapter 17	Quest	page 166
Chapter 18	Responsibility	page 173
Chapter 19	Sales	page 180
Chapter 20	Team	page 204
Chapter 21	Universal laws	page 213
Chapter 22	Value	page 224
Chapter 23	Will	page 230
Chapter 24	Xcuses	page 235
Chapter 25	Yo-yo	page 241
Chapter 26	Zest	page 247
Epilogue		page 257
Winners		page 265
Notes		page 295
Photos		page 324
About the Author		page 337

DEDICATION –

Dedication [ded-i-key-shuhn] *Origin:* late 14c., "action of dedicating," from Fr. dédication (14c.), from L. dedicationem, noun of action from dedicare (see <u>dedicate</u>). Meaning "the giving of oneself to some purpose" is c.1600; as an inscription in a book, etc., from 1590s.[1]

Dedicate [ded-i-keyt] *Origin*: late 14c., from L. dedicatus, pp. of dedicare "consecrate, proclaim, affirm," from de- "away" + dicare "proclaim," from stem of dicere "to speak, to say." Dedicated "devoted to one's aims or vocation" is first attested 1944.[2]

- • -

I FORMALLY OFFER MY DEEPEST TESTIMONY of affection and respect to the following people:

To my children, José Luis II ("JL"), Laura Grisel ("Lori"), and Alexis Liset ("Lexi"). You always inspire me to be better.

To my wife, Maria Elena. You helped me dream again when you entered my life. I love you.

To my father, Homero Hinojosa. You have always been a caring provider and you are worthy of emulating. Thank you, dad.

To my mother, Rosalinda F. Hinojosa. You continue to guide me from the Heavens, each and every day. I miss you, mom.

Acknowledgments –

Acknowledgments [ak-nol-ij-muhnts] *Origin*: 1585-95, a blend of M.E. aknow (from O.E. oncnawan "understand," from on + cnawan "recognize;" see <u>know</u>) and M.E. verb knowlechen "admit." Somehow, in the merger, a parasitic -c- slipped in, so that, while the kn- became a simple "n" sound (as in know), the -c- stepped up to.[3]

- • -

I WOULD LIKE TO THANK ANYONE WHO'S EVER HAD A DREAM and has found the courage to go after it. Because of you, individuals like me get the opportunity to share our passion with the world. I am ignited and I do believe it's contagious...so use your best judgment from this point forward.

I also thank all the successful individuals, all the winners, and mentors whose ideas, teachings, wisdom, knowledge, and language contributed to this book. You will find their names in alphabetical order after the Epilogue, each with a short description.

I especially thank my good friend, Presley Swagerty, for honoring this book with his winning personality, charisma, and knowledge... and, of course, for writing the Foreword. ¡Gracias, amigo!

FOREWORD –

Foreword [fohr-wurd, -werd] *Origin*: 1842, perhaps a loan-translation of Ger. Vorwart "preface," modeled on L. præfatio "preface."[4]

Also, a short introductory statement in a published work, as a book, especially when written by someone other than the author.[5]

- • -

WHEN JAY-EL ASKED ME TO WRITE THE FOREWORD for this amazing book, I was honored. Recommending *The Language of Winners*! allows me to introduce Jay-el Hinojosa and his teachings to some people who might not have had the opportunity to get to know him.

Over the years, I have had the good fortune to spend some quality time with Jay-el and have found him to be a winner in every area of his life. Whether it's business, family, or martial arts, he is a champion.

His unique insights and storytelling make this a rare book that can be read and understood by anyone. Each chapter contains a different fundamental that Jay-el has identified as essential for winning. You will study each fundamental through a combination of quotes and anecdotes, ending with a personal game plan that will help you be a winner. No matter where you are in your life, these fundamentals are timeless and will give you great training.

It is my personal goal to add value to people's lives on a daily basis – Jay-el shares this same goal. If you study the principles he shares in this book, and use them, you will benefit greatly by reading *The Language of Winners*!

~ PRESLEY SWAGERTY
Nationally acclaimed networker and
author of *Millionaire by Halftime*

Preamble –

There is no "i" in team, *but there is in* win.

~ Michael Jordan

Preamble [pree-am-buhl] *Origin*: late 14c., from O.Fr. preambule (13c.), from M.L. preambulum, neut. adj. used as a noun, properly "preliminary," from L.L. præambulus "walking before," from L. præ- "before" + ambulare "to walk" (see amble).[6]

- • -

I WALK BEFORE YOU SO THAT I MAY STAND before you and set forth the following general principles of **The Language of Winners!**

In a perfect world, a child is born out of love. And one of the very first things this child will do in the delivery room is cry. He may belt it out or he may not, but regardless, he's just announced his arrival. Over and above the formal announcement, the neonate is fully expanding his baby lungs with that first cry. However, after that initial cry, a baby has no other way of communicating with others...except for crying. For a baby, crying is synonymous with the most basic of human interactions: communication.

But, what is the baby saying when he cries? Is he hungry, soiled, ill, uncomfortable, too hot, too cold, tired, thirsty, sleepy, in pain, colicky, or does he simply need to be held? With patience and love, the parents will be able to understand what certain cries mean, and how to better fulfill the baby's needs. That's right, there *will be* different cries. The pitch, the tone, the volume, the frequency, and even the crying pattern are ways the baby will communicate.

As babies grow, their verbal and nonverbal language foundation will grow as well, as they add more and more approaches to their communication skills. More skills means more effective communication; less skills means your needs are not met, your relationships suffer, and your self-image takes a punch in the gut.

According to Joel Osteen, "one of the best ways we can improve our self-image is with our words."[7] He believes words are like seeds in the sense that they have creative power. Joel also quotes the scriptures as saying, "We will eat the fruit of our words,"[8] which means that our words produce that which we are saying. Yet another scripture says, "With our tongue, we can either bless our life or we can curse our life."[9] Therefore, we must be extremely cognizant of what we choose to say because "our words set the direction for our lives" and declaring good things, speaking blessings over your life will not only help you develop a better self-image, "but you will become a better you."[10]

But verbal communication is (surprisingly) only a small fraction of the total communication picture. By far, the biggest part of communication for humans is body language, or nonverbal communication. Your body's posture and your facial expressions speak louder than words. An extension of this is the adage "A picture speaks a thousand words." The way you stand, the way you carry yourself, and the way you look at someone paints a certain picture – a picture that conveys a much louder message than the words that are coming out of your mouth.

Joe Navarro, a nonverbal communication expert and former FBI agent, says that "up to 80% of what we communicate is nonverbal."[11] A person with any amount of influence over others must, therefore, realize that his followers are watching. This leader is a role model, whether he knows it or not. Others are watching your actions, and they're doing as you're doing...even when you strongly encourage them to "do as I say, not as I do."

According to UCLA Psychology professor, Dr. Albert Mehrabian, we relate to people in three V's: *verbally* (with words), *vocally* (tone of voice), and *visually* (body language). He says that body language tells the truth, even when our words lie. "If there's an inconsistency between the verbal, vocal and visual, our words give off the least information," says Dr. Mehrabian. "Our facial expressions play the greatest role."[12] Thus, every eye blink, every eyebrow raise, every lip smack, every raised corner of the mouth, and every facial twitch speaks volumes. And he who speaks the best wins.

Speaking of UCLA and winning, UCLA coach Henry Russell ("Red") Sanders said the following in a 1950 football workshop: "Men, I'll be honest. Winning isn't everything." A long pause followed, and then he concluded his thought with, "Men, it's the only thing!"[13] At the outset, the coach let everyone know he is not willing to settle for anything but the best. It's his attitude, it's his mentality, it's a certain *je ne sais pas* that makes him a winner. And winners not only make themselves great, they make those around them great – they *surround themselves* with greatness.

Winners have an obvious spring to their gait, an irrefutable oozing of confidence through their pores, a veritable glow to their faces, and a specific manner of connecting and communicating. That's right; winners have a language all their own – **The Language of Winners!** And, regardless of your mother tongue, it is my desire that this book will become a sort of *lingua franca* memorialized within these pages.

More than about winning, **The Language of Winners!** is a book about individuals who have defied the odds and about how they impart their message to others. The words they use, the tone they use, and the body language they use to overcome their obstacles or their adversaries. Verbal, vocal, and visual indications are the tools. The arena, on the other hand, is any and all – it can be a sports field, a boardroom, a fancy restaurant, a fast-food establishment, a school classroom, a local park, a popular tourist attraction, or even your home.

Of course, to be a winner, to succeed at anything you do, you need more than just a set of tools and a place to utilize them. You need to understand not only **what** specific tools to use for the greatest impact, but also **when** to use them, **where** they should be used, **how** to use them, and more importantly, **why** you're using them and with what *feelings* and *purpose*. Zig Ziglar says that "your attitude, not your aptitude, will determine your altitude." Thus, when studying the language used by winners, you must realize "there is little difference in people, but that little difference makes a big difference. The little difference is attitude. The big difference is whether it is positive or negative." ~ W. Clement Stone.

A great attitude will not only bestow upon you opportunities others only dream of, it will also ignite the fire of your imagination. And imagination is what created this book, this *child* born out of love – out of my love to inspire, to contribute, to make a difference, to teach, to enlighten, and to improve your life. Today, this book is bigger than my imagination, bigger than a simple idea; today, this book is a reality, it is tangible. And because it is tangible, you can touch it, you can study it, you can read it, you can turn the pages until there's no more to turn, and you can place it atop your other personal development books as yet another step in your Personal Improvement ladder.

That's what **The Language of Winners!** is – it is a step, an instrument, a tool of specially-selected words, sounds, and gestures used as a means of communicating winning emotions, winning thoughts, and winning ideals to YOU, the reader, the most important person in the world. Thus, you can continue your quest for personal growth, for knowledge, for development, for improvement, for inspiration, and even perhaps, for illumination.

It is my heartfelt desire that you quickly adopt a winner's stance – raise your arms to the heavens, tilt your head up, and puff out your chest[14] – and show the world you're a winner. And once you've integrated this type of posturing, all you have to do to maintain your winning ways is to continuously learn, become fluent in, and habitually speak... **The Language of Winners!**

Have a blessed read.

José Luis "Jay-el" Hinojosa, MD

PS - I'd love to hear how ***The Language of Winners!*** is contributing toward your personal and financial success. Just log on to **www.TheLanguageOfWinners.com** and share your success story online... or, for a more personal touch, simply write to me at:

P.O. Box 3550
Edinburg, TX 78540

ALPHABET –

Actions, looks, words and steps form the alphabet by which you may spell character.
~ Johann Kaspar Lavater

Alphabet [al-fuh-bet, -bit] *Origin*: 1560s (implied in alphabetical), from L.L. alphabetum (Tertullian), from Gk. alphabetos, from alpha + beta, the first two letters of it, from Heb.-Phoen. aleph, pausal form of eleph "ox" + beth, lit. "house;" the letters so called because their shapes resembled or represented those objects. The Greeks added -a to the end of many Heb.-Phoenician letter names because Gk. words cannot end in most consonants. Alphabet soup first attested 1907.[15]

- • -

ALL LANGUAGES SHARE AN IDIOSYNCRASY with each other. They allocate a nucleus, a core, an alphabet, or a system of basic facts and figures that represents and identifies their particular language. ***The Language of Winners!*** is no exception. Winners who are, or wish to be, fluent in their specific language of triumph, success, victory, conquest, and achievement must adhere to their simplest fundamentals – their ABCs.

Here then, is the alphabet formed by **The Language of Winners!** – with an inspirational quote followed by a brief description of its origin at the beginning of each chapter.

A is for **Attitude.**

> A winning attitude is your pleasing state of mind with regards to some*one* or some*thing*; it is the engaging physical posture you adopt that expresses what's inside of you. Everything else being equal, attitude is the difference maker.

B is for **Believe.**

> Winners believe in themselves first, then in what they represent – their team, their company, their product, or their service. Winners have a strong conviction; they believe deeply in their heart and soul that they have what it takes to succeed.

C is for **Call me!**

> Winners make themselves available and they are there when you need them. They are just a phone call, a text, or an e-mail away. Winners encourage others to call for assistance or to ask questions because it is a sign of strength, not of weakness.

D is for Discipline.

Discipline allows you to follow-through with what you have started. To you, discipline means daily activity, practice, and preparation. As a winner, you polish your skills, techniques, and presentations so that you can continue your winning ways.

E is for Education.

Winners are continuously learning and growing. They refuse to settle; they are not yet satisfied with their accomplishments. Winners realize that an education, especially self-education and personal growth, can take you to the top of the success totem pole.

F is for Focus.

Winners focus on what's important to others first, and then to what's important to them. They converge, zoom in, and concentrate on what needs to be done now. Winners understand that great amounts of concentrated effort are more powerful than a laser beam and that focus will allow them to reach their destination quicker.

G is for Giving.

Winners are givers, not takers; and they give more than what is expected. Because of their generous nature, winners are philanthropic, altruistic, and great humanitarians; they willingly give back to society.

H is for Habits.

Winners have a dominant disposition of achieving their goals; their temperament is that of success. Winners are in the habit of winning – and winning habits come naturally to them because they've practiced them over and over again.

I is for Insults.

Winners do not let offensive actions or words get them down; they turn insults into compliments. Winners can spin disrespect into respect faster than a chicken can cluck "fowl" language.

J is for Just right!

Winners perform precisely, flawlessly, and to the letter. They go to great lengths to be exact and completely accurate in their words and actions.

K is for Kinetics.

Winners accept *action* as the operative word in their formula for success; they understand they have to "get moving" in order to reach the top of the mountain. Winners plan their work, and then they *work* their plan.

L is for Leadership.

Winners are leaders who exert influence over others; they are leaders because they are role models that others emulate. As leaders, winners do what others are unwilling or unable to do in order to succeed.

M is for Mannerisms.

The appearance of winners is that of being in control; they stand a certain way, they walk a certain way, they simply carry themselves with confidence. Winners display the characteristics that tell the world, "I'm here! Let's do this!"

N is for Network.

Others have a job and they go to work, but winners build and develop massive networks. Winners engage a support system of like-minded individuals who dedicate their efforts at networking, instead of "not working."

O is for Options.

Winners have worked diligently so they can have options in life, so they can make choices others only dream of. Winners are prepared to recognize when an opportunity comes knocking, and they immediately capitalize on it.

P is for Patience.

Winners display the capacity to endure delays or provocation without getting their feathers ruffled. Tenacity, persistence, and perseverance allow winners to outlast everyone else. Winners get up, dust themselves off, and try again – and losers never do.

Q is for Quest.

Winners are on a mission, and others know it because they see it in their eyes. Winning is about the journey, not the destination. Winners are in search of self-improvement and self-realization, while simultaneously searching for ways to be of service to others.

R is for Responsibility.

> Winners are responsible for their actions and they hold themselves accountable for their results. Because they are capable of rational thought and actions, winners have the ability to choose their responses to what life throws at them.

S is for Sales.

> Winners are consummate salespeople; they sell themselves first and foremost. Once your prospect and audience buys into you, they will buy into whatever it is that you, as a winner, represent.

T is for Team.

> Winners work well with others; they elevate the level of everyone around them by bringing value to the team. Winners recognize that Together, Everyone Achieves More.

U is for Universal laws.

> Just as the sun always rises in the east, winners predictably rise to the occasion. Winners excel in maximizing results and minimizing set-backs by accepting and collaborating with the laws of the Universe.

V is for Value.

> Winners assist others by allowing them to help themselves; they bring value to others by being of service and delivering more than is expected. Winners make themselves useful in every scenario.

W is for Will.

> Winners have the drive, desire, and determination to see the job done to completion. Hungry winners are never satiated because their resolve will never allow them to give up.

X is for Xcuses.

> Winning is not about pointing fingers or blaming others for the reasons you did not succeed. Winners make money and make things happen; they do not make excuses.

Y is for Yo-yo.

> Winning is not about "yo, yo, yo" (Spanish for "me, me, me") – winning is about "you, you, you." Winners think of others first by empowering them in a systematic fashion; they realize that the best way to reach the top is to bring others with you.

Z is for Zest.

> Winners enhance everyone's appreciation of life; they share their unique energy and vitality. Simply put, winners enjoy an animating spirit, an enthusiasm, and an extraordinary interest for everything they do.

Chapter 1

ATTITUDE – Part I

You cannot control what happens to you, but you can control your attitude toward what happens to you. And in that, you will be mastering change rather than allowing it to master you.

~ Brian Tracy

Attitude [at-i-tood, -tyood] *Origin*: 1660–70; < French < Italian *attitudine* < Late Latin *aptitūdini-* (stem of *aptitūdō*) aptitude.[16]

Aptitude [ap-ti-tood, -tyood] *Origin*: 1540s, "quality of being fit for a purpose or position," from L.L. aptitudo (gen. aptitudinis) "fitness," noun of quality from L. aptus "joined, fitted" (see apt).[17]

- • -

WHEN I WAS A PRACTICING FAMILY PHYSICIAN, my mother, Rosalinda Fernández de Hinojosa, was diagnosed with the one thing that had haunted her throughout her life, the one thing that instilled fear in her, the one thing that had taken her own mother's life when mom was only 10 – the big "C." In fact, for a long time she couldn't even bring herself around to say the word "cancer."

Mom and dad lived alone in south Texas. All six of their kids, now adults, lived in different parts of the state. One evening, mom was taking a shower when she slipped and fell, injuring her right wrist. My father, Homero Hinojosa, took her to the local hospital in Eagle Pass where she was told, after 3 hours in an empty Emergency Room, "Yup, it's broken." My mom smiled and in her typical composed persona, advised the staff that she knew it was broken, that's why she was there. She showed them the extra step in her wrist and with continued restraint, said that she did not go there to be told what she already knew – she went there to be treated.

When she was advised that the closest Orthopaedic Surgeon was in San Antonio (about a 3-hour drive), my parents decided instead, to take the 2-hour trek to Laredo and try their luck there. Apparently, Laredo was also devoid of Orthopods, so mom and dad made the decision to seek a bone doctor in México. They crossed international waters into my birth city, Nuevo Laredo, where a cast and a sling were promptly applied, and they were sent on their way.

Around 10pm that night, as I was getting ready to retire for the evening in my home in McAllen, I got the phone call. It was my father; he narrated the events that led to the call. When he mentioned that mom's hand was swelling up and she couldn't feel her fingers, I told him to bring her over right away. He did.

A little after 3:30am, I met up with my parents at my clinic in McAllen. Mom's fingers were inflated like a red balloon that was about to pop! At this point, her entire upper extremity was completely numb. Luckily, I had the necessary equipment for removing casts and was able to saw off the offending vise rather quickly. Mom sighed with relief and gave me a kiss on the forehead, like she always did. She was now starting to get some life into her hand.

Because the rational thing was to wait about a week for the swelling to go down before another cast would be attempted, my wife suggested we do some routine exams on mother. Why not? Everyone agreed it was a wise move, since mom was going to be staying with us for a while, anyway. Dad, always the responsible type, drove the 5 ½ hours back to his obligations at Texas Finance Company as soon as the sun came up.

And so it was that a very early incidental finding on a routine mammogram was identified. My friend and surgeon extraordinaire, Dr. Jesus Rodriguez, wasted no time; he scheduled her for the Operating Room right away. I was the surgical assistant to Dr. Rodriguez when the diagnosis of AdenoCarcinoma of the breast came back from Pathology. It would mean more surgeries, radiation, and chemotherapy...all of which made her additional chronic conditions of Type II Diabetes Mellitus and Hypertension all the more ominous. I, however, was fortunate to be present in all her subsequent procedures and treatments.

And then came the big one: Dr. Rodriguez told mother and me that 1 in 500,000 will get a "side-effect" to the radiation therapy, a secondary effect, a more aggressive cancer, a cancer that has no treatment, a so-called AngioSarcoma – and mom was that *one in five-hundred thousand.* It never ceases to amaze me but through it all, mother maintained a positive attitude. And just as Dr. Jesus Rodriguez is a master surgeon, she was a master herself...of seeing the glass half full instead of half empty, of finding the good in the bad, of counting her blessings instead of her disappointments. Not once did she say *why me?* Never a negative thought, a negative action, a negative word. Many came to me in awe of mother's always-optimistic mind-set. Yes, she had a knack for seeing the bright side of things.

Mom fought the cancer for more than 15 years until January 19, 2005 at 4:05am, when she could fight no more. That, by the way, is also the exact time and date that my youngest sister, May, was born forty years earlier. Countless individuals approached May and told her what a bad omen this was and that they were sorry she would have to deal with this the rest of her life. But May has internal fortitude and a great attitude – she learned from the best – and she saw mom's timing as a great honor, as an unparalleled privilege. Mom said good-bye when she did for a reason, and as she departed this world and entered another, she left behind her "attitude of gratitude" legacy to her children. Mom always taught us to thank God that we are alive. And I believe little sis inherited more than just a great attitude from mother – my sister had the ultimate torch passed on to her, the torch of a grateful, optimistic, and happy outlook on life. What a tribute! I am so proud of both of them.

Rosalinda Fernández de Hinojosa, my mother, lived her life with a winning attitude despite many years of pain and suffering due to ill health. When others complained about minor inconveniences, mom rejoiced in the face of major setbacks. Zig Ziglar put it this way: "Of all the attitudes we can acquire, surely the attitude of gratitude is the most important and by far the most life changing." How true. And whenever my mother walked into a room, the place lit up with her optimistic radiance. How ironic that instead of her being at the receiving end of encouragement, she was the one lifting the spirits of her healthy counterparts!

Rosalinda Fernández de Hinojosa was a winner with an attitude of gratitude because she innately understood... ***The Language of Winners!***

ATTITUDE – Part II

You are the average of the five people you spend the most time with.

~ Jim Rohn

My wife, Maria Elena, bought me the book, *The Five Major Pieces to the Life Puzzle,* by America's foremost business philosopher, Jim Rohn. In the book, Mr. Rohn says that how we *feel* about our way of thinking determines our attitude.[18] The way *I* felt after receiving that gift from my wife was grateful, loving, animated, and I was definitely all smiles. You know, I've heard that a happy wife means a happy life. Well, I believe that a happy husband is not too bad, either.

So, attitude is identified by Jim Rohn as one of the five main areas in life. He says that how we feel is influenced by our associations – that's why he advises that winners need to continuously ask themselves three questions:[19] 1) Who am I associating with?, 2) What effect are they having on me?, and 3) Is this acceptable to me? In other words: Who am I around?

What am I *saying* now that I'm with them? What are my *actions* now? What *books* am I reading, if any? What films or television programs am I watching? What am I *thinking* since I started being around them? And more importantly, Who am I *becoming* by being associated with them? Finally, is that okay with me?

Of course, by constantly gauging your associations, you can make sure that you are able to recognize and eliminate the negative influences in your life, while connecting and engaging with the positive ones. It is up to you; you decide.

In *Twelve Pillars*, the novel Jim Rohn co-wrote with Chris Widener, one of the characters explains it this way: "Surround yourself with winners, successful people who exhibit and live consistent to values and skills you want to acquire and develop. You see, the people in your life have an amazing power to influence your destiny."[20]

Three extremely positive people in my life who have influenced my destiny and who understand how associations can sway your attitude in one direction or another, are:

- My Grand Master in Tae Kwon Do, Hong Kang Kim, would remind our class that, "Birds of feather, flock together!"[21]
- My mother always said, "Dime con quien andas y te diré quien eres." (Translation: "Tell me who you are with and I'll tell you who you are.") And she would follow it

with, "Bic" – as in "be careful." That was the extent of her English.

- My good friend and multi-millionaire entrepreneur, Presley Swagerty, would say the following variation of mom's Spanish adage to his high school basketball team: "Tell me who you hang with and I'll tell you who you are or who you're gonna be."

All three impart sage advice. Presley alludes to the fact that although you may be subject to inferior, mediocre, or plain ole' bad influences, you can still change for the better – you still have hope. And if your sphere of influence is unwilling to acknowledge the winning attitude you bring to the table, then maybe you should reconsider and think about associating with new people. Jim Rohn says, "If you can't change your friends, then *change* your friends."

Remember, you cannot choose your relatives, but you *can* choose your friends. Choose positive, successful, enthusiastic, go-getters and do yourself a favor. It will definitely have a positive impact on your future. Epictetus, the Greek philosopher, believed that "The key is to keep company only with people who uplift you, whose presence calls forth your best."

Winners feel empowered and they transmit this to others. But they are also vulnerable to negative influences. That's why winners should frequently assess, reassess, and evaluate their associations by: 1) listing their closest relationships, 2) reflecting on who they are becoming as a result of those relationships, and finally, 3) by deciding if they are willing to tolerate their transformation. Winners dedicate time to analyzing their friendships, their associations, their contacts – and in so doing, winners can design a brighter future for themselves and for those they care about.[22] Winners can do this because they've learned to change their associations, when needed, and to enhance their language to... **The Language of Winners!**

Chapter 2

BELIEVE –

The future belongs to those who believe in the beauty of their dreams.

~ Eleanor Roosevelt

Believe [bih-leev] *Origin*: 1150–1200; Middle English *bileven,* equivalent to *bi-* be- + *leven,* Old English (Anglian) *gelēfan* (cognate with Dutch *gelooven,* German *glauben,* Gothic *galaubjan*).[23] O.E. belyfan "to believe," earlier geleafa (Mercian), gelefa (Northumbrian), gelyfan (W.Saxon) "believe," from P.Gmc. *ga-laubjan "hold dear, love" (cf. O.S. gilobian, Du. geloven, O.H.G. gilouben, Ger. glauben), from PIE base *leubh- "to like, desire" (see love). Spelling beleeve is common till 17c.; then altered perhaps by influence of relieve. To believe on instead of in was more common in 16c. but now is a peculiarity of theology; believe of also sometimes was used in 17c.[24]

- • -

In the early 1980s, the karate tournament circuit in the U.S. was ruled by my good friend, Keith Vitali. *Black Belt magazine* actually considered Keith as one of the top ten karate fighters of all time.[25] I asked him what, besides his great looks and awesome kicks, made him so successful and he told me, "Jay-el, every time I went to a tournament I took two uniforms with me." In those days, martial arts uniforms were pretty standard – mainly all white, although some other colors were starting to show up in competitions. "Two," I said, "why two?" Keith smiled and then added, "One for the eliminations, and one for the finals."

Keith was so confident in his abilities, in all the time he had put in at the dojo (martial arts school), that he was determined to look like a winner, to look sharp both in attire and in technique during the championship bout. He believed with all his heart he was supposed to be there, he believed he belonged, and he believed he would win...and more often than not, he'd win it all!

After learning of Keith's two-uniform approach, I began to do the same – it was simply brilliant. Every night before a major tournament, I would visualize every single technique, every kick, every punch, every block that would take place the following day; I would picture my opponents failing; I would see *and feel* my hand being raised as the winner, as the tournament champion! I envisioned all these details about the next day's events while I performed, what I call, my *Iron Relaxation Techniques*. I would review all of this in my mind's eye while ironing my two uniforms – it was therapy, it was so relaxing, and it got me into the proper frame of mind for the next day. I believed in what I was doing and it paid great dividends.

Of course, there's no substitute for practice, practice, practice. A lot of people say, "Practice makes perfect." The way this adage stands, it's not completely accurate – because you can practice something *wrong* for twenty years and it doesn't mean you are going to get any better at it, does it? I always tell my martial arts students that "perfect practice makes perfect!" You commit to performing the task, the technique with correct form, timing, rhythm, power, and focus… and only *then* can practice make perfect!

I took this advice to heart during the Amateur Athletic Union's (AAU) National Tae Kwon Do Championships of 2006 in Knoxville, Tennessee. I did not show up alone – my two loyal companions were a world-class level of physical conditioning and preparation. And before the National Anthem was played over the speaker system, I lined up with the rest of the 1,658 athletes. I remember closing my eyes and visualizing my techniques, my power, my focus, even my win, while the melody played on. As my hand was raised, the anthem finished. It was simply perfect timing! Everyone clapped, and I opened my eyes, ready to conquer that tournament, that day.

As I searched for a spot to warm up and stretch, I recognized a fellow winner. It was Peter Bardatsos, a former Team USA member whom I had the pleasure of caring for during several World Championships overseas. As he approached me, he looked surprised and said, "Doc, you compete?" With a smile, I said, "Of course, Peter. And you know what? I'm winning the Gold today!" Peter showed his pearly whites, tapped me on the shoulder, and wished me luck. He hurried off in search of his pupil he was about to coach and mentor.

My division that day was the largest of the entire National Championships – there were 68 competitors vying for 4 spots: Gold, Silver and 2 Bronze. It was a *Poomse* competition, similar to a dance-for-your-life routine, where you perform a choreographed fight against imaginary opponents. Two at a time performed on the 8x8 meter competition area, and as my luck would have it, the athlete that competed alongside of me had a huge cheering section that began making noise even before we were given our starting signal. I, on the other hand, had what I considered to be the *home field* advantage. True, none of my supporters were *physically* present at the venue, but that did not deter me. The hard work had already been done at the gym – today would be nothing compared to that.

The command was given and, like two thoroughbreds, we bolted out of the starting gates. I fought just as I had seen myself the night before during my therapy session and during the National Anthem at the start of the competition. Intensity, focus, and power were ubiquitous on my side of the mat. My kicks powered through the air, my punches snapped on impact, and my breathing was perfectly synchronized with my movements. I was alone – the other competitor on the mat, Mr. Jones, did not exist.

When we finished, we were given our scores by the four corner judges and the three on the head table. The high and the low scores were dropped, as always, and we were dismissed. When we sat outside the competition area, Mr. Jones was dumbfounded. He breathed effortlessly when he spoke to me and said, "I can't believe you scored higher than me!" In between breaths, I answered, "I can!" His look was equally astonished, and as my respirations continued to labor, I said, "Look at you – you're not even breathing hard. I, on the other hand, well... *(catching my breath)* I was fighting for my life out there!" He did not say another word. His eyes, on the other hand, spoke volumes – they told me, "You're right. You were willing to die out there...and I wasn't."

The planets were aligned that day, as I won the Gold by a landslide! Later on, as I admired the Gold medal around my neck, Peter once again ran into me. He stopped me and, with a huge smile, said, "Hey Doc, you said you were gonna win the Gold...and you did!" He gave me a congratulatory embrace and

I was glowing the rest of the day!

Someone else who was probably also "glowing" after his win was David, as in the Biblical story of David & Goliath. As you know, Goliath was a giant who was terrorizing the townspeople for 40 days and 40 nights. Nobody wanted to stand up to him; the common feeling was that Goliath was too big to hit. In *Zig Ziglar's Spiritual Journey*, Zig tells us that David thought otherwise; David figured Goliath was too big to miss![26] The whole difference was the point of view: the townspeople looked at Goliath and compared him to them, and he looked awfully big. However, David looked at Goliath and compared him to God, and he looked terribly small. Evidently, David's belief in God allowed him to defeat Goliath.

And when Zig Ziglar finished telling this story to his 7 year old son, he added, "Son, wasn't David a brave boy?" The child answered, "Yeah, Dad, David was brave...but Goliath was the brave one." Dumbfounded, Zig asked his son to explain his comment. The young Ziglar spoke as a person much older and much wiser, as he said, "Well, Dad, you've got to understand...Goliath was out there right by himself. David had God with him!"[27]

Just as Zig shared with his son, so do I with my kids; I tell JL, Laura, and Alexis that if you want to accomplish something you just have to remember the ABCs, only backwards. CBA stands for the words that W. Clement Stone uttered years ago,

"Whatever the mind of man can **c**onceive and **b**elieve, it can **a**chieve." Those are the ABCs backwards, although I modify it a bit and put in some action so that it's easier to remember. I say, "What your mind can *conceive,* and your heart can *believe,* you will *achieve!*" The movements added to this are: 1) touch your temples with your index fingers of both hands when you say "conceive," 2) cross your hands over your heart when you say "believe," and 3) with your index fingers starting at eye level and to your sides, do one loop with each going away from your body, and end up like a symphony conductor when you say "achieve." This latter movement is sign language for *accomplish* or *succeed.*

Nothing can stand in your way if you first conceive it in your mind, if you think it, if you visualize it as real; next, if you believe it in your heart, if you believe it in your soul, if you believe it with all your might; and finally, you will achieve your dreams, you will accomplish your goals, you will fulfill your destiny, you will succeed – because you saw to fruition that which was merely an idea or a thought. Think of belief as the bridge between idea and success.

Of course, there are those who advocate that "seeing is believing." They are on the skeptical side, they are slow to change, they resist progress – and thus, they need "proof" prior to fully committing their time or effort. They think their eyes will guide them to the Promised Land. I propose that the opposite is true – "believing is seeing." I reiterate: once you truly believe with your heart and soul, then your eyes will see with a clarity that wasn't there before. It will all be so obvious...if you first believe.

Personal improvement experts remind us that significant wins have actually been accomplished twice – once in your mind, and once in real life. You have seen that particular success twice, every single time. I advocate taking it a step further – I believe that winners accomplish everything three times; winners see every one of their wins thrice! Winners first see with their mind, then they see with their heart, and finally they see it with their eyes in real life...because believing is seeing. That's why the heart of a winner, the soul of a winner, first and foremost believes in...***The Language of Winners!***

Chapter 3

CALL ME! –

Life is like a game of cards. The hand that is dealt you represents determinism; the way you play it is free will.
~ Jawaharlal Nehru

Call [kawl] *Origin*: 1200–50; late Middle English *callen*, probably < Old Norse *kalla* to call out, conflated with Old English (West Saxon) *ceallian* to shout; cognate with Middle Dutch *kallen* to talk, Old High German *kallôn* to shout, akin to Old English *-calla* herald, Irish *gall* swan, OCS *glasŭ* voice.[28]

Me [mee] *Origin*: before 900; Middle English *me*, Old English *mē* (dative and accusative singular); cognate with Dutch *mij*, Old High German *mir*.[29]

- • -

NOTHING SAYS, "I'M SERIOUS ABOUT MY BUSINESS," like a professionally designed business card. It is your calling card. It says to the world, "I'm available. I'm there for you. I can find solutions to your problems. So, call me at your convenience." As a customer, I get peace of mind whenever I have access to someone whom I can call with questions or concerns. This availability quickly translates to ongoing trust. And we all know that people do business with people they like, people they trust, and people that make them feel good. Bottom line: Business cards are an inexpensive way to boost your business! Thus, I always provide new contacts with my business card.

Imagine you are experiencing side effects to a medication prescribed by your doctor…and you can't find his number so he can tell you what to do! Say, you were trying to reach your family doctor and you couldn't. You believe your condition is not bad enough to dial 911, but you still want your doctor's advice…and he's nowhere to be found. You get the Answering Service and half an hour later you get a call back from an Assistant or someone else who's on call for your physician, and this Someone Else has no idea about your medical history. He doesn't know what medication you were prescribed and you can't remember where you left the bottle.

And then you get a lucky break – you remember the name of the Pharmacy that dispensed your medicine! So, now Someone Else is able to start doing some investigative work. He calls the Pharmacy, but it is Saturday night and there are two other physicians on the line, ordering meds. He is put on hold for a while, and when he finally gets the name of the medication you are on, he calls you back. It is now another 35 minutes later – more than one hour since your initial call.

In that hour, you start getting worried, and you start thinking of all the terrible things that could be wrong with you. Then, your anxiety level climbs. Your pulse speeds up. You start to take quick, shallow breaths. You blow off too much carbon dioxide – and now, you are hyperventilating. There's no brown bag to breathe into, so you get light-headed and you pass out. Your head hits the hard floor first – the rest of your body follows. Now, you have a head injury and the prognosis just got worse. All this because somebody wasn't available for you. Perhaps all you needed was his business card!

During most of my medical career, I *personally* answered my patients' after-hours calls. My physician colleagues were shocked I followed this *modus operandi*. They all used Answering Services. In the beginning, as a new physician, I too used an Answering Service because I thought that's what I was supposed to do. However, I found that I could better serve my patients if I answered their calls directly. Plus, I got fewer and fewer calls (despite a growing practice) as my patients got more and more educated on the signs and symptoms to look for. They also had the reassurance that I was literally a direct phone call away, ready to ease their pain, which brought them peace of mind. At the end of the day, what I discovered through this approach was that my patients' anxieties, for the most part, were relieved the moment I answered the phone. It was almost magical!

Common sense told me that if you are doing business, you show the world you are serious about your business and you hand out your business cards. But then again, as the Old Chinese proverb goes, "Common sense - not so common." So, I was under the impression that handing out business cards was simple, common sense and common practice. That is, until I met some peculiar folks. Here's what happened –

Some time ago, I attended a business luncheon hosted by a company that was courting me so I would buy their product. During a recess, I approached several of the speakers because I wanted to follow-up with them. When I asked 2 or 3 of them for a card, they all said almost in unison, "We are not card givers, we are card collectors!" I had never heard of such an animal, but apparently the room was full of them. So, in order to save face, one of the more proactive speakers quickly went to another table, borrowed an 8 ½ x 11 sheet of paper and a pencil, and wrote his name and cell number on it. He proceeded to place it on my table and we continued to talk. After the short intermission was over, it was back to the meeting so everyone took their seats. And then, the inevitable happened - someone on my table spilled a cup of coffee and the hot liquid took no 8 ½ x 11 prisoners! The paper was soaked and the contact information was smeared to illegibility.

The speaker saw this from his neighboring table and, since he wasn't on stage at the moment, he scrambled for another paper, quickly re-penciling his information all over again!

When I asked him to please explain once again why he did not believe in business cards, he said, "My time is very valuable and I have to be really selective about who I talk to on the phone. If I don't have a business card, I can't give one away, and people can't call me whenever they please! As a card collector, people give me their business cards and I get to choose when I talk to them!" His company's associates who were close enough to hear this, nodded in agreement. All I saw were the bobbing heads of the Card Collectors, that new toy I had just been introduced to. I hoped it would not catch on.

Manipulative, untrustworthy, unfair, insidious, selfish, and egocentric are just some of the words that came to me. If even a few of these words find their way to the prospect's mind, surely this can't be good for the Card Collectors' business.

So, what's the best way to hand out your business card? The answer is: there are many ways. One thing you do not want to do is simply give them out to everyone. It turns out that if there's no compelling reason for your prospect to hold on to your card, he will just get rid of it. Next!

In my 25+ years of doing business, I've heard many techniques for handing out your business card. Here's the great Jim Rohn, in one of his many audio programs, sharing a very creative approach when you're at the checkout counter, paying for goods:[30]

Jim Rohn: Have you found the opportunity that will take care of you and your family for the rest of your life?

Clerk: Uh, I didn't even know there were such opportunities.

Jim Rohn: Well, then I have to ask you another question. How much *time* do you spend each week *looking* for it?

Clerk: I didn't even know I should be looking!

Jim Rohn: Well, when you *decide* to start looking, here's my card. Give me a call.

What Jim Rohn is really saying to the clerk in the opening query is that there are opportunities out there that can change the clerk's life, the lives of her children, and her children's children, for generations to come. So, when the clerk admits she wasn't aware that this was even possible, Jim Rohn's follow-up question about *time* and *looking* gives urgency to the whole scenario. It is really saying, "You should already be looking, Missy!" When the clerk, again, admits she didn't know any better, she will realize there are opportunities that she hasn't even considered; opportunities that other people are already taking advantage of. In addition, she may experience fear of missing out on something great, or fear of loss. Maybe she will feel that her lack of action now is associated with a devastating loss at some later time.

But Jim Rohn did not do a "hard sell." He did not pressure her into acting *now before this promotion ends and it's gone forever!* He simply reinforced that it is *her* decision to make, and when she *does* make it and decides to call, he will be there. A great example that couples fear of loss with urgency…and without the car-salesman pressure! This is yet another reason why Jim Rohn is a master.

Here's another approach I really like. It is by Michael Bernoff, from his *Progress in Action* webinars.[31] He has a technique whereby your prospects will just about *beg* for your business card. He recommends rejecting your prospect first! That's right, the moment something happens to a person that he doesn't expect, it remains in his memory forever. In a way, it is *ingrained in his brain!*

Before you hand your prospect your card, pull it back and say, "I'm going to give you this with one condition." So now, your prospect's hand is outstretched and all he can do is reflexively say, "What? What's going on?" You continue, "Will you commit and take ownership that when you get home, you'll send me an e-mail? Because, most people say they're going to do something and they don't. That's not you, is it?"

Well, your prospect is so taken by what you are doing that he will not want to be *the person* who let you down. So, he will answer, "Of course not!" Then you say, "Okay, you can have it." And you have just handed your business card to a prospect that now doesn't want to let you down.

In his book *The Brand Within*, Daymond John gives some advice on how your business cards can stand out from the competition and make you more memorable. He recommends using *blind embossing* on your business cards so that at first, your prospect may not notice it, but then he will be forced "to pay just a little more attention to who you are and what you're about."[32] He also recommends making your cards a little bit bigger or a little bit smaller than the standard size – that way, your card will not go on the usual pile and people won't be able to help but notice you. Not only will you be showing your innovative side, you will also come to mind before everyone else because you impressed your prospect.

Well-designed, creative, professional business cards in the hands of qualified prospects, customers, patients, or business associates, invariably say, "I've got your back. I've got the answers to your questions. I've got fresh ideas to take your business to the next level. I'm just a phone call away."

It is easy to see why business cards are a portable, simple way to convey... ***The Language of Winners!***

Chapter 4

DISCIPLINE –

Discipline is the bridge between goals and accomplishment.
~ Jim Rohn

Discipline [dis-uh-plin] *Origin*: 1175–1225; Middle English < Anglo-French < Latin *disciplīna* instruction, tuition, equivalent to *discipul* (*us*) disciple + *-ina*.[33]

Disciple [dih-sahy-puhl] *Origin*: O.E. discipul (fem. discipula), Biblical borrowing from L. discipulus "pupil," from *discipere "to grasp intellectually, analyze thoroughly," from dis- "apart" + capere "take"[34]

- • -

THE WORDS "HOUSE OF DISCIPLINE" are boldly exhibited in many martial arts schools where I've trained, or visited, around the world. And because the word "martial" refers to "military," martial arts are military arts. "The military history of the martial arts," as I reveal in my book *Tae Kwon Do for Everyone*, "maintains a foundation in today's martial arts training."[35] It is precisely this discipline that many parents are looking for when they bring their child to a martial arts school. They want the child to obey commands; they crave the child starts acting in accordance with the rules; they hope the child will learn to respect authority; they fancy that this activity will develop some desirable skills in the child; they yearn for the child to learn self-control and not get into trouble any more.

The summer of 1982 was my last "free" summer during medical school; after that, I was to attend school without breaks or interruptions in good o'le Cincinnati until my graduation in 1985. That summer, I spent it with my parents in south Texas and I worked two jobs: I was an orderly during the night shift at the Maverick County Hospital and I taught martial arts during the day at a local gym. But my students weren't just any students; they were a dozen of the meanest little kids you would ever come across. They were 10-12 year old delinquents and trouble makers. They were *The Little Dirty Dozen!*

Their parents brought them to me almost as a last resort, so that I would straighten them out, if I could. I took on the challenge and during the first few weeks, they would come in to class boasting about what fight they got into earlier in the day, or about what kid they had just bullied. And although I did not know it at the time, I followed Jim Rohn's teachings of being "strong, but not rude; kind, but not weak; bold, but not a bully; thoughtful, but not lazy; humble, but not timid; proud, but not arrogant; have humor, but without folly."[36] According to *Twelve Pillars*, these "bad characteristics are just good ones taken to the extreme and used for selfish reasons."[37]

They started to change – it was as if they were a ball of clay and I was molding them into good little boys. Pretty soon, they would come in to class sharing their success stories about how they avoided a confrontation and about how they did not need to fight anymore! "We did what you taught us," they would say with a big smile. "And how did you feel when you walked away?" – I asked with genuine interest. "Great, coach!" – they would answer. "We felt great, coach!" I had never been called "coach" before.

At the end of my three months with them, that dirty dozen, those twelve little hoodlums, were now *good* kids. On our last day together, they surprised me with pizza, chips, and soft drinks. We had a wonderful farewell party, we took lots of pictures, and even their parents participated. It was very gratifying!

As evidenced from this story, the *discipline journey* can go from zero to hero quite fast. Lao Tzu reminds us that "the journey of a thousand miles begins with a single step." That first step was the parents bringing their children to the class.

The children took all the other steps themselves; they stayed on course and they were engaged in the learning process. Thus, the sometimes long and winding road of discipline can start with the non-existent discipline of trouble makers who start their quest of obedience and growth, and it can end up with the outstanding discipline of world-class athletes, as in my next story.

I was fortunate to have served our US National Tae Kwon Do team as official Team Doctor between 1993 and 1998. The fact that I am also a Tae Kwon Do practitioner gave me deeper understanding of these athletes during my tenure. I was a sort of *Players' Doc* (as opposed to a Players' Coach); I was someone who could relate. In fact, many of our athletes were actually shocked that I could fill-in and train with them, when needed. They were used to non-athletic doctors in prior years.

During that time, I traveled all over the globe treating our elite athletes and our coaching staff – nobody was immune. From applying splints, slings, and wraps; to fitting crutches; to stitching up lacerations; to removing foreign bodies from eyes and ears; to bringing down fevers; to treating sinusitis, cystitis, acute gastroenteritis, and other words that end with *–itis*; to diagnosing pregnancy, I can honestly say that Sports Medicine addressed more than athletes and their sport.

In retrospect, I can honestly say that my time as Team Doctor was one of my defining moments during my 25 year medical career. Not only was this volunteer work very rewarding professionally, but also on a personal level. Professionally, I was privileged to care for elite athletes who are the epitome of discipline, plus I got to experience first-hand the medical systems in place in other parts of the world, like the Philippines, Brazil, Hong Kong, and South Korea. Personally, I developed some great friendships with both, athletes and coaches.

In one of our trips to South Korea, a Junior Team (ages 14-17) member hurt his foot during warm-ups. I watched as he kicked, landed awkwardly, and then limped to the back of the line. When it was his turn again, he wasn't able to perform – and that's when I intervened. As I walked toward him, and because I had witnessed the actual mechanism of injury, I felt I already knew the diagnosis. I was able to immediately put my finger on it, literally. I palpated the base of the 5th metatarsal on his left foot and he grimaced in pain. When I advised the coaching staff that I believed our athlete had fractured his foot, everyone thought I was kidding. They laughed and wanted him to continue with the drills.

After a while, calmer heads prevailed and I was able to persuade the coaches into allowing us to go for an x-ray. We took a cab to a local hospital, where patients filled all the seats in the Emergency Room's waiting area. When it was finally our turn, I introduced myself to the physician on duty, a pleasant man, and then waited for the x-rays to get done. Both physicians concurred with the diagnosis of fracture. There was an interruption of the osseous structures at the base of the 5th metatarsal bone, on the outside of the foot, and this was pointed out and explained to our athlete. *(Note: What a contrast from my mother's visit to the Emergency Room. We were actually cared for quicker in a foreign country, with a busy E.R.!)*

The diagnosis of fracture was brought back to the coaching staff and I remember someone saying, "Good, so, it's not broken, right?" It seems that coaches prefer that their players continue, instead of the opposite. I explained that a break, a crack, a chip, and a fracture are the same, just different ways of saying it.

I am reminded of a story Darren Hardy, publisher of *SUCCESS* magazine, tells about his father, who was a college football coach and strict disciplinarian. Coach Jerry Hardy demanded a lot from his players. One day, his quarterback asked to come off the field due to an injury and the Coach said something to the tune of, "You're not coming out unless you're showing bone!" So, the player pulled at his shoulder pad and revealed a bone protruding out of his skin.[38] He was allowed to go out, but nobody else could...unless they were *showing bone*. (In medical parlance, he had suffered a *compound fracture,* a very ominous sign that carries with it increased potential for infection and other complications.)

Discipline is hard work because it consists of ongoing, daily activity…and only a select few are willing to undergo its rigors. In *Twelve Pillars*, the novel by Jim Rohn and Chris Widener, one of the characters asserts, "We must all suffer from one of two pains: the pain of discipline or the pain of regret. The difference is discipline weighs ounces while regret weighs tons."[39]

At or near the end of our lives, winners will celebrate all the beautiful moments they shared with their loved ones, they will be proud of all the successes they were able to accomplish, and they will experience fulfillment at all their dreams they were able to pursue. On the other hand, individuals who allowed fear to stop them on their tracks – who did not risk following their dreams and passions – won't be celebrating anything in their deathbeds, they will feel ashamed of all the opportunities they allowed to slip through their fingers, and that's when they will experience the brunt of the enormous weight of the pain of regret.

Winners suffer the tiny pain of discipline, which is nothing compared to that of regret. Winners learn and develop new skills, where perhaps there were none. Winners engage in a strict regimen in order to improve their technique, when they already enjoy good form. Winners focus and travel the road called discipline – yet, even those without discipline, those who lack direction and guidance, those who've been in trouble in the past, can travel on this road... all it takes is small, daily actions and you can get to the success finish line. Zig Ziglar reminds us that "it was *character* that got us out of bed, *commitment* that moved us into action, and *discipline* that enabled us to follow through."

Discipline is a daily activity, an exercise, a regimen that improves and develops... **The Language of Winners!**

Chapter 5

EDUCATION – Part I

Great leaders are never satisfied with ordinary. *They want to do* something, *or say* something, *or be* something *that just is a little bit bigger and a little bit better than what average is...so that they are attractive to others and they are adding value to others in a way that is uncommon.*
~ John C. Maxwell

Education [ej-oo-key-shuhn] *Origin:* 1525–35; (< Middle French) < Latin *ēducātiōn-* (stem of *ēducātiō*), equivalent to *ēducāt* (*us*) < Latin *ēducātus* brought up, taught (past participle of *ēducāre*), equivalent to *ē-* <u>e-</u> + *-duc-* lead + *-ātus*.[40]

- • -

IT WAS 1995 AND THE COUNTDOWN HAD STARTED. The place was the Philippines. Manila, to be precise. I glanced at the clock – seventeen seconds! Sixteen! Fifteen...

Come on, almost there! I was trying to "will" the second hand to go faster. Years of dedicated, hard work had boiled down to the last few seconds of the final round, Round 3. *Not out of the woods yet,*[41] I thought. Fourteen seconds...

Our team, the U.S. National Tae Kwon Do Men's Team, is about to win its very first *ever* Gold Medal in a World Tae Kwon Do Championship! Even more remarkable is that it is taking place far from home, without the home-court advantage one always aspires to have during an important sporting event such as this one. We are halfway around the world and the only cheering section we can muster is our own team! As the clock winds down, the decibel level winds up as more and more people realize what is about to happen. They are watching history in the making. They are watching the Thrilla in Manila,[42] Part 2.

Our athlete, Jean Lopez, hails from the great state of Texas and his opponent, José Jesus Marquez, a slightly taller fighter, represents Spain. The clock continues. Thirteen seconds... for the grueling match to be over! As the official doctor for our USA Team, I was there a few feet from the action, cheering our fighter from *the inside* – not so much from *the outside*, since "cheerleaders" were frowned upon that close to the fighting area. I had to do what my profession taught me; I had to keep cool, calm, and collected. With Jean ahead by one point and only 12 seconds separating him from Gold, it was now only a matter of time. He just needed to start running – out – the...

WHAM!

The 11 second mark! It came out of nowhere! The two stood there, in a clench – the Spaniard looked validated and the Texan looked utterly confounded, even comical, as his headgear had shifted on his vertex and covered his eyes.

What just happened? Well, at that nano-instant, my heart skipped a beat and Jean's probably stopped altogether. He was the epitome of an athlete who was ahead one second, and then he wasn't. This image was courtesy of an incredible kick to the head – and I still can't believe it! And just like that (*snap of the fingers*), Spain was up by one.

The representatives from all 77 countries understood the importance of a kick to the head, especially in a closely contested match. Head kicks are worth 2 points, one more than any other technique in Olympic-style Tae Kwon Do in 1995. And then, somebody pushed the fast-forward button – and the final 11 seconds went by like a flash: kick, block, double kick, counter-kick, parry, side-step, grab, punch, evasion, frustration for one, ecstasy for another, and the eventual buzzer that signaled... "Stop!" And that was it.

Oh, the agony – of losing, of having to "settle" for second, of having the Gold slip through your fingers! Or perhaps, the thrill – of winning the Silver medal, of being one of the top 2 athletes in the world, of going out there and "grabbing" 2nd place from the rest of the field! The end result in these two descriptions is still the same: a Silver medal winner. However, it depends on how this experience is communicated, that will ultimately reveal one's true perception of what really happened. It is the point of view that matters. How one looks at it. How you interpret and react to what's going on around you. You see, the experts tell us that we cannot control what happens around us, but we *can* control *how we react to what happens*.

John C. Maxwell, America's foremost authority on Leadership, mentions a mathematical formula that he learned in the 70s from Earl Nightingale.[43] The formula is: E + R = O (read, "E plus R equals zero"). In other words, an "event" (E) takes place at or near you; it will elicit your "response" (R), which will in turn yield an "outcome" (O). Of course, since many times we cannot control the event (e.g., a natural disaster, like a tornado – or, as in this case, a "tornado-like" kick that caught us all by surprise), and if we want to change the outcome, we will have to change our response. So, what was Jean's response? How did this athlete react after this gut-wrenching match was over? He reacted like a winner!

I happened to walk into Jean's room that night when he was on the phone with someone from Texas – his father. Jean was going over the play-by-play from the Gold Medal match. Toward the end of the conversation, he said something that confirmed to me he's a winner. He said, "How do I feel? I feel very happy with my effort...but I'm not satisfied. No, I'm not... yet... satisfied." He said it in a calm tone and demeanor. To me, he uttered those last three words, not – yet – satisfied, on the down stroke of a metronome set at 45 beats per minute. The bradycardia of an athletic heart. He was in synch *and* he was serious. Not upset, not complaining. He was voicing his truth, his expectations. He was making an affirmation – to his father, to me, to the world – and he meant it.

Fast-forward again to the present day. Today, Jean is the Head Coach of the USA Olympic Tae Kwon Do team and his three younger siblings (Steven, Mark, and Diana) have not only been guided and coached by big brother, but they've also garnered a plethora of Olympic and World Championship medals – including the one that got away with 11 seconds to go! In fact, under the elder sibling's mentorship, the Lopez trio claimed a sort of *revenge* (and made history in the process) by each winning the Gold Medal at the 2005 World Tae Kwon Do Championships in (where else?) Spain! Even more impressive is that the total Gold Medal count for the USA that year was...exactly three![44]

Despite all their victories, if you speak to the Lopez', that essence of a true winner is still there. What will resonate now is what resonated that November night in a hotel room in Manila: *I'm not yet satisfied*. The Lopez', like most winners, want more – because if they were satisfied, it would put an end to their hunger, to their desires, to their dreams. To be satisfied is to have all your wants, needs, dreams and expectations *completely* fulfilled. Thus, you would not want more. Were it thirst, it would be quenched; were it hunger, it would be satiated; were it a book, you would close it and it would start collecting dust on a shelf in a book cemetery. You would start to become complacent. And one who is complacent loses the winner's edge – in fact, one who is complacent will probably *never* experience the winner's edge!

The Lopez siblings will take you to school because they kick hard, they kick fast, and they speak... **The Language of Winners!**

EDUCATION – Part II

An investment in knowledge pays the best interest.
~ Benjamin Franklin

MOST ADULTS UNDERSTAND THE IMPORTANCE of a formal education. We want our children to receive the best education possible because we want them to do well, we cheer for their success, we look forward to hearing all about their dreams and aspirations, and we pray that they "graduate." Children represent the future. In fact, my family immigrated to America for that very purpose – to have the opportunity to acquire an education that could open the doors of endless possibilities.

The level of commitment required to do well during the educational process is astonishing. Studying and doing homework is hard work. If it was easy, everyone would proudly display their college diploma on their wall, but that's not the case. Hispanics, for instance, account for less than 6 percent of all recipients of bachelor's degrees in the United States![45] It's not that easy.

I remember when my mother owned and operated Hinojosa's Grocery, a small neighborhood store in south Texas. It was an early autumn day in 1978 when one of the neighbors, who was around my age, dropped in to purchase a toothbrush, some toothpaste, a comb, a razor, and one of his staple foods, a six pack of beer. Since mother had not seen him for a while and he looked disheveled, she asked what had become of him. He answered, "Estaba en la grande." (Translation: "I was at the big one." He was referring to prison.) Mother asked why and he said, "Porque me filarié a uno." ("Because I sliced up a guy.")

After he purchased his items, he looked around and did not see my brother or me, so he inquired, "Where are your sons? Are they working?" At the time, my brother Juan Homero and I were attending Brown University in Providence, Rhode Island and mother said, "Yes, they work very hard." "Oh, yeah? Where do they work?" Mother then answered with great pride, "They're at the University." He made a dismissing motion with his hand, "Ahhh, that's not work! That's school!" My mother said, "Well, school *is* very hard work. Why are *you* not in school?" He turned around and left, popping the top of one of the cans.

In 1980, when I graduated from Brown, Hispanics accounted for only 4 percent of all college students nationwide![46] That means that if 100% of Hispanics successfully graduated from college in 1980 America, only 4% of us would have received a college degree. In fact, a major, multi-year study found that "Hispanics lag behind all other racial/ethnic groups in the rate at which they earn a bachelor's degree."[47] Thus, going to school and earning a college degree *is* very hard work – my mother was right.

Jim Rohn, like my mother, was a big proponent of education. In a classic recording from the November 2009 *SUCCESS* CD, he said, "Books are the trademark of civilization."[48] He believed we should continue reading, especially *after* finishing the educational process because a "standard education will get you standard results" and because "a formal education will make you a living; self-education will make you a fortune." He was referring to life-long learning, not just reading and learning during your years in school, but actual personal growth and self-improvement – things that are not taught at school.

In the August 2010 *SUCCESS* CD, Darren Hardy asked the great Brian Tracy what he would consider to be the keys to continuous, life-long learning. Brian Tracy answered like the master he is – he said that all great truths are simple. And simplicity dictates that the cumulative effects of these three keys to life-long learning will yield astounding results: 1) *read* one hour per day in your chosen field; one hour per day is one book per week, which translates to 50 books per year, which will put you way ahead of everyone else, 2) *listen* to educational and personal improvement audio programs in your car, especially when the average person drives 500-1,000 hours/year; and 3) *plug-in* to as many personal growth and development seminars and courses as you can; being around like-minded, success-oriented individuals will only fuel your winning ways.[49]

Darren Hardy reminds us that spending ten percent (10%) of your income on personal improvement will be the best investment you can make; the return on investment (ROI) will be astonishing. So, shoot for the moon – and if you don't get there, you'll land amongst the stars. That's why I believe in education; first, get your degree, then continue with life-long learning… because a formal education can teach you about the Solar System, and self-education will allow you to discover the Universe.

Winners are readers, and readers are leaders. Winners are life-long learners, and life-long learners are life-long earners. Winners are constantly learning – at home, in the car, and in virtual and live seminars; they are committed toward not only academic progress, but also toward personal growth and development. Winners understand that a commencement ceremony doesn't signal the end, it signals the beginning – the beginning of a life-long quest for knowledge. In his book *Success for Dummies*, my mentor Zig Ziglar says it like this: "Every time you take a step forward by learning something of value, you improve your picture of yourself. Because that picture determines your performance and your performance determines your future, the daily acquisition of knowledge and skills is a marvelous way to ensure your future."[50]

So, take a step forward by learning something of value. And by doing so, you will be on your way to becoming a winner. That's right, winners are consummate learners, they are relentless at ensuring their future, and they earn high interest rates for their knowledge and expertise because they bring value to others via ... **The Language of Winners!**

Chapter 6

FOCUS –

Remember that a person's name is, to that person, the sweetest and most important sound in any language.
~ Dale Carnegie

Focus [foh-kuhs] *Origin*: 1635–45; < Latin: fireplace, hearth.[51] 1640s, from L. focus "hearth, fireplace," of unknown origin, used in post-classical times for "fire" itself, taken by Kepler (1604) in a mathematical sense for "point of convergence," perhaps on analogy of the burning point of a lens (the purely optical sense of the word may have existed before Kepler, but it is not recorded). Introduced into English 1650s by Hobbes. Sense transfer to "center of activity or energy" is first recorded 1796. The verb is first attested 1814 in the literal sense; the figurative sense is recorded earlier (1807).[52]

- • -

PEOPLE ARE SAID TO MANIFEST A "SWEET TOOTH"

when they crave sugar-filled morsels. My son, J.L., for example, always lights up in the presence of chocolate-chip cookies. He has a fondness for that sugary, chocolaty stuff. And as he grew from childhood into adolescence, his tooth got the best of him…and he succumbed. He wandered into foreign territory, the kitchen, and took matters into his own hands. J.L. cooked his own cookies – and, of course, he ate them! Now, as an adult, he bakes the cookies and shares them with everyone.

Just like there's a sweet tooth, there's also a "sweet ear." The sweet ear is undeniably more of a challenge to satiate properly than the sweet tooth. It can certainly be accomplished, but somewhat inconsistently. The sweet ear is an innate occurrence and you get to experience it when you hear that delightful sound, your name. Your name, when pronounced correctly, is very pleasing to your ear and your soul. It is almost magical. Thus, winners focus on what's important to you – you and your name.

On the other hand, when someone says your name incorrectly it tends to disagree with you such that it produces an unpleasant bitterness of the ear and sourness of the soul. It can definitely upset you! And the culprit, the mispronouncer, may not have the slightest clue as to what just happened. He may have done it innocently enough, but you may have perceived it as malicious. I know I get uncomfortable when someone calls me *José or Hosea*, instead of *José Luis* or *Jay-el*, my stage name. *José* doesn't feel right; there's something missing. My good friend, Jim Wagner, is probably the only person who can call me *José* and get away with it. We met when we were both teens, during a difficult time in both of our lives, so when he says my name it strikes a *sincere chord* within me that reverberates throughout.

In his 1936 best-selling, self-improvement book *How to Win Friends and Influence People,* Dale Carnegie gives several examples of why it is important to remember and use people's names. He says that there is magic in a name and that we should be aware of the fact that the sole owner of that name is the person in front of us at that precise moment. The name is what makes that person feel important, unique, and special. He is not just a number any more, he's somebody with an identity and he matters. Mr. Carnegie says that whatever it is that we are communicating to that person, if his name is used when we approach him, the circumstances will take on a special magnitude.[53]

Some of Carnegie's techniques for remembering people's names still hold true today. Namely, when Napoleon III, Emperor of France, was asked how he could remember the name of every person he met, he answered that he concentrated on the name and repeated it several times during the initial meeting/conversation, and tried to associate the new name in his mind with specific features, expressions, and appearance of the person he just met.[54]

I learned the 2011 version of Napoleon's technique at a Personal Improvement conference in Dallas, Texas. Ron White, twice USA National Memory Champion, was a keynote speaker at the event and I remember seeing him meeting and greeting people before he took the stage. Since I had never seen Ron before, I did not know what to expect. However, I guesstimated that he was probably going to get to the stage and impress everyone by remembering people's names.

Profuse sweat covered him and he was clearly in a hurry when I made a dash for him, but he was quicker than I. I remember wondering how he ever got away from me – maybe he used some Jackie Chan moves to maneuver himself around the thousands of attendees. That's it, Jackie Chan defeated me – Ron White did not! If one of my friends heard that a non-athlete left me, a world karate champion, in the dust I would never hear the end of it – if Jackie Chan left me in the dust, that's easier to swallow.

At any rate, my hand shake and introduction that never happened would have revealed my true name: *José Luis Hinojosa Fernández Guerra Ramón*. As you can imagine, in my mother land of México, we use all the last names! Ron White would have truly impressed me if he remembered my name that evening.

Granted, with all those last names I possess, and in a foreign tongue, it is going to be more difficult to remember. Would you agree then, that it is hard to remember something you do not understand? Of course it is. That's why, if you did not understand your new acquaintance's name, you should ask him to repeat it. If it's an uncommon name and you still can't get it, perhaps you can ask him to spell it for you. And once you are confident you have the correct name, spend some time, focus, and memorize it. Practice, practice, practice. After that, you should archive it in a "file" specific for that person, or that event in which you met, *within* your memory library. If you do this, your files will be organized and easy to retrieve whenever you need them. With this method, my file in Ron White's memory would have been something like, "gray-haired, pale-skinned guy without eyebrows, with very long Hispanic name." Perhaps he would go as far as pasting my name on an imaginary U.S. flag, and start singing the Star-Spangled Banner, "Oh, José, can you see...that you have no eyebrows!" Voilà, Ron White would have successfully remembered my name!

That day, Ron White effectively remembered the names of two-hundred people he had just met – two-hundred! I was there! However, he *did* struggle with a few. And what did he do with those he had a difficult time with? He literally walked up to them, studied their faces with intense focus for a few seconds, and then he was able to recall their names.

I remember vividly when my NeuroAnatomy professor, Dr. James B. Hall, announced to our medical school class, "As humans, we are visual beings." This was his introduction to our study of the brain's occipital lobes, the visual cortex. It is in the visual cortex, in the back of the brain, where all visual information is processed. And, how many times do you hear people say, "I never forget a face, but I'm terrible with names."

Isabel Gauthier, Associate Professor of Psychology at Vanderbilt University, co-authored a study that shows we can remember more faces than other objects because of the way faces are encoded. Faces tend to "stick" better to our memory banks. Kim Curby, from Yale University and the study's primary author, compares encoding to packing a suitcase. She says, "How much you can fit in a bag depends on how well you pack it. In the same way, our expertise in 'packaging' faces means that we can remember more of them."[55]

This study also revealed that objects (i.e., cars and clocks) were remembered better than faces when the test subjects were given half a second to study the images. However, when more time was given (specifically, four seconds) to encode the images, faces were remembered better than objects. Thus, faces can be remembered better if we only focus on someone's face for a mere 4 seconds! I believe that's about how long Ron White spent focusing on the hard-to-remember people's faces before he came up with the correct names.

Actors, on the other hand, face different challenges – those of remembering their lines. They can better remember their lines once they've done the blocking, once they've figured out their movements on stage, as opposed to when they only have a script in their hands. With this approach of tying-in words to movements, you can enhance your memory. You can go directly to your file for this particular theatrical production in your memory library because you are organized.

I was one of the lead actors at a community theatre production earlier this year when I used this technique. I couldn't remember my lines during a particular scene, and then I realized that once Toñita handed me the glass of lemonade, I would stand up and tell the actor to my left, "Come, Rufas! Let me show you that new rooster that hatched a couple of weeks ago!" And then I would step with my left foot forward, stop, and turn to my right to deliver my next line to Toñita. And that's how you can perform an entire 2 ½ hour play without notes – by connecting your movements to your words.

One of my early acting teachers, Dr. Marian Monta, always stressed the importance of blocking and movements on stage. When someone would forget a line, she would say, "What business are you doing?" (In the theatre, the term "business" is when you keep busy on stage, it is incidental action such as taking a sip of the lemonade. It's mainly done to make the character more realistic – but it also helps with remembering lines.) And once the actor grasped what business he needed to perform, he would go "off book" earlier because he learned his lines quicker. Dr. Monta also directed me in some of Shakespeare's works, which were slightly more challenging because nobody speaks that way in today's world. Thus, when our blocking allowed us to better understand what was meant by that soliloquy, the Shakespearean terminology now made sense, and the lines flowed with that *iambic pentameter*[56] rhythm from our mouths.

Coming back to Ron White's version of Napoleon's methodology for remembering names, here's an example of what Ron shared during the conference. Let's say the person you've just met is Steve. Steve sounds like stove, so get an image of a stove in your head and paste the name "Steve" on the stove. Next, paying attention to Steve's appearance, you notice that he has an unusually large nose – focus on that. And because we tend to remember better when words are associated with actions, he recommends you grab that stove and shove it up Steve's schnozzle. Perhaps this is a bit graphic, but next time you see Steve you will probably remember his name and you will use it at all the right moments in the conversation. Steve, as you can suspect, will be amazed that you hold him in such high regard. He may, in fact, want to send you his business in the near future.

Winners are especially adept at focusing on your sweet ear by remembering and using your name appropriately. In this way, your interactions with them will always be gratifying and productive. And why shouldn't they be? Winners have succeeded in touching your soul in a very special, yet simple, way. You can do the same; just put in a little bit of concentrated effort and technique the next time you meet someone. Pretty soon, you will remember people's names as if they were part of your family and you will beat the rest of the pack in regards to business deals, even if only by a nose, because you have focused on mastering... **The Language of Winners!**

Chapter 7

GIVING –

We make a living by what we get, but we make a life by what we give.

~ Winston Churchill

Giving [giv-ing] *Origin*: before 900; Middle English < Old Norse *gefa* (compare Danish *give*); replacing Middle English *yeven, yiven*, Old English *gefan, giefan;* cognate with Dutch *geven*, German *geben*, Gothic *giban*.57 I believe it is when you are unselfish with your gifts, talents, time, and effort – and in the process, you bring value to others.

Give [giv] *Origin*: O.E. giefan (W. Saxon), class V strong verb (past tense geaf, pp. giefen), from P.Gmc. *gebanan (cf. O.Fris. jeva, M.Du. gheven, Ger. geben, Goth. giban), from PIE *ghab(h)- "to take, hold, have, give" (see habit). It became yiven in M.E., but changed to guttural "g" by infl. of O.N. gefa "to give," O.Dan. givæ. Meaning "to yield to pressure" is from 1577. Given "allotted, predestined" (O.E. giefeðe) also had a n. sense of "fate," reflecting an important concept in pagan Gmc. ideology. The modern sense of "what is given, known facts" is from 1879. To give (someone) a cold seems to reflect the old belief that one could be cured of disease by deliberately infecting others.[58]

- • -

ARE YOU A GIVER OR A TAKER? Do you give more than you get? Winners give of themselves, they care about others, and they are generous with their time, effort, commitment, and love. They give back to society not because they *have* to, but because they *want* to.

Jim Rohn says that "giving is better than receiving because giving starts the receiving process." The key is that when you give without any expectations that the receiver is obligated to you in any way, your rewards will be even greater than the original amount. Some experts say that your R.O.I. is ten times what you gave.

One of *TIME* magazine's 25 most influential Americans in 1996, Stephen Covey, has a solid view of giving back. He says, "Financial success – prestige, wealth, recognition, accomplishment – will always be secondary in greatness. Primary greatness is about character and contribution. Primary greatness asks, *What are you doing to make a difference in the world? Do you live truly by your values? Do you have total integrity in all of your relationships?*"[59] Stephen Covey is saying that your medals, trophies, diplomas, and wins are good, but they are only secondary victories. Giving back to society is the true victory for winners.

In 1986, during the second year of my Family Medicine Residency training in McAllen, Texas, I started volunteering as Team Doctor for one of the local high school football programs. At first, I showed up on Saturday mornings, during the Athletic Trainer's evaluations of the injured players from the night before. The head coach, Alex Leal, was thankful that I was there and that I was offering my expertise. One day, he finally said, "Hey, doc – why don't you just join us as our team's doctor. You're always here, anyway!" Of course, I said yes. I thought I would help out for a season or two – in the final tally, I was there 13 years!

I started out with one high school, and as the games expanded from Friday nights to include Thursdays and Saturdays too, I ended up on the sidelines of three or four different schools. Many times, I would cover the teams of other physicians, when they were unavailable. And when injuries outnumbered the volunteer physicians on hand, I would spend half a game in one venue and the other half at another venue. Usually only one ambulance covered the games, so when it wasn't on stand-by because it was en route to the hospital and another player got injured, my car was the back-up ambulance. I literally drove scores of athletes on Friday nights to the Emergency Room. I could usually tell when I was going to be especially busy: when I rushed for more yards than my team! Running from the sidelines to the middle of the field during an injury time-out, and then back, multiple times during a game, tends to pile up your yards. That's good for your stats on total yards...*if* you're a running back, not a doctor!

Friends and acquaintances who found out I was the doctor at Friday Night's games would ask, "What number is your son?" They would ask this, because 99.9% of physicians on the sidelines before my time were there because their son or nephew was on the team. When I answered that nobody from my family was playing, they could not believe it. Yes, it was very hard work, but I enjoyed every minute of it. I did not get paid in money, I got paid in peace of mind and always having a great night's rest – well, when I wasn't delivering babies in the middle of the night.

Speaking of football, N.F.L. Hall of Famer Jim Kelly and his wife, Jill, welcomed the birth of their son, Hunter, with great expectations in 1997.[60] However, at the age of four months, Hunter was diagnosed with Krabbe Disease (or *Globoid-Cell Leukodystrophy*), a rare and fatal nervous system disorder that affects the brain. Krabbe Disease prevents the development of significant motor skills and children afflicted with it only live about 18 months – Hunter reached 8 ½ years of age!

Jill Kelly says, "We were both living the kind of life that celebrity football families live, with all the material things we could ever want. Then Hunter came into our life, and he saved our family. God used him to help us see the greater purpose in our life. He used this little boy who couldn't speak a word to speak volumes into our life and into the lives of families like ours."[61]

The Kelly's started a non-profit organization, *Hunter's Hope Foundation*, the same year their son was born.[62] It has raised millions of dollars to help fund research and innovative treatments, and it hopes to assist the medical establishment in eventually finding a cure for Krabbe Disease. As an ongoing tribute to Hunter, the Foundation has helped pass legislation to improve newborn screenings for earlier detection and treatment. Already, thousands of families have benefited from The Kelly's legacy of giving.

Stories of pain, suffering, and philanthropy like The Kelly's bring to mind an adage by Lao Tzu, which says, "Kindness in words creates confidence; kindness in thinking creates profoundness; kindness in giving creates love." And it is common scientific knowledge that not only do the recipients of good deeds experience improved health and well-being, but so do the givers.

A connection between altruism, unselfishness, and self-sacrifice, and stress relief was accidentally found in 1956 by a group of researchers from Cornell University in New York City, when they followed 427 married women with children, for 30 years. The researchers assumed that the women with more children would have more stress and die earlier than their counterparts with fewer kids, but the results were astounding; they found that 52% of the women in the study who did not volunteer suffered a major illness, compared with 36% of the women who *did* volunteer![63]

Giving, altruism, and philanthropy have more to do than just handing out money. The amazing Oprah Winfrey says, "I don't think you ever stop giving. I really don't. I think it's an on-going process. And it's not just about being able to write a check. It's being able to touch somebody's life." Oprah is a winner who makes a difference in many people's lives, and when you do that enough times, you will come face to face with the so-called *helper's high*. The *helper's high*, that euphoria you experience after performing a good deed, is believed to have a scientific foundation.

Stephen G. Post, PhD, a professor of bioethics at Case Western Reserve University School of Medicine, says that Magnetic Resonance Imaging tests have been used to identify certain areas of the brain that are extremely active during deeply empathic and compassionate emotions. Dr. Post says, "These brain studies show this profound state of joy and delight that comes from giving to others. It doesn't come from any dry action – where the act is out of duty in the narrowest sense, like writing a check for a good cause. It comes from working to cultivate a generous quality – from interacting with people. There is the smile, the tone in the voice, the touch on the shoulder. We're talking about altruistic love."[64]

Likewise, the beneficial effects of giving go beyond the neuro-psychology of generosity; they directly tap into the immunology and endocrinology components, as well. Dr. Post goes on to cite a large research study that found a 44% reduction in early death among volunteers – a greater effect than exercising four times a week![65] Wow! Perhaps if you volunteer *and* exercise, you will get even more formidable results.

Winners give and give and give, without expecting any ROI. It turns out winners get and get and get, more than anyone thought. Your generosity as a winner will allow you to live longer, healthier, and happier because you have given from your heart and soul, and you are making a difference in the world. Yes, when you authentically give back to society, you are the true winner because you have selflessly shared...***The Language of Winners!***

Chapter 8

HABITS –

We are what we repeatedly do. Excellence, therefore, is not an act but a habit.

~ Aristotle

Habits [hab-its] *Origin*: 1175–1225; Middle English < Latin *habitus* state, style, practice, equivalent to *habi-* (variant stem of *habēre* to have) + *-tus* verbal noun suffix; replacing Middle English *abit* < Old French.[66]

- • -

SAGE ADVICE IS A TIME TRAVELER that leaves a positive impression whenever and wherever it goes. In the year 2012, one may not want to consider advice from a grocery store owner named Ernest in 1940 America. Unless, of course, his last name is Buffett – as in Warren one-of-the-wealthiest-men-in-the-world Buffett. Then, perhaps, that advice can be taken as gospel. Ernest was Warren's grandfather and in 1940 he wrote the same letter addressed to each one of his children. Thirty years after the letter was written, Warren Buffett discovered it in a safe deposit box along with the cash mentioned in the letter. The following, addressed to Fred, Warren's uncle, and Fred's wife, is that letter:[67]

Dear Fred & Catherine:

Over a period of a good many years I have known a great many people who at some time or another have suffered in various ways simply because they did not have ready cash. I have known people who have had to sacrifice some of their holdings in order to have money that was necessary at that time.

For a good many years your grandfather kept a certain amount of money where he could put his hands on it in very short notice.

For a number of years I have made it a point to keep a reserve, should some occasion come up where I would need money quickly, without disturbing the money that I have in my business. There have been a couple occasions when I found it very convenient to go to this fund.

Thus, I feel that everyone should have a reserve. I hope it never happens to you, but the chances are that someday you will need money, and need it badly, and with this thought in view, I started a fund by placing $200.00 in an envelope, with your name on it, when you were married. Each year I added something to it, until there is now $1,000.00 in the fund.

Ten years have elapsed since you were married, and this fund is now completed.

It is my wish that you place this envelope in your safety deposit box, and keep it for the purpose that it was created for. Should the time come when you need part, I would suggest that you use as little as possible, and replace it as soon as possible.

You might feel that this should be invested and bring you an income. Forget it — the mental satisfaction of having $1,000.00 laid away where you can put your hands on it, is worth more than what interest it might bring, especially if you have the investment in something that you could not realize on quickly.

If in after years you feel this has been a good idea, you might repeat it with your own children.

For your information, I might mention that there has never been a Buffet who ever left a very large estate, but there has never been one that did not leave something. They never spent all they made, but always saved part of what they made, and it has all worked out pretty well.

This letter is being written at the expiration of ten years after you were married.

Ernest Buffett

"Dad"

This is what Warren Buffett said in 2011 of his grandfather's timeless financial advice:[68]

> *At Berkshire, we have taken his $1,000 solution a bit further and have pledged that we will hold at least $10 billion of cash, excluding that held at our regulated utility and railroad businesses. Because of that commitment, we customarily keep at least $20 billion on hand so that we can both withstand unprecedented insurance losses (our largest to date having been about $3 billion from Katrina, the insurance industry's most expensive catastrophe) and quickly seize acquisition or investment opportunities.*

Like Ernest and Warren Buffett, a short Mexican man by the name of Homero believes in putting a cash reserve aside, just in case. Homero is my 87 year-old father. He did not complete an elementary school education, he only speaks Spanish, and he has worked hard all his life. In fact, for the past 50+ years, he has gone to his office like clockwork, Monday through Friday, at a small Loan Company without ever taking a vacation. He has had opportunities to rest, but he told me that he can rest later. He also advised me that to succeed, you have to be consistent with your actions; your actions have to become a habit. Dad has told me many times, "A través de los años, he desarrollado un solo hábito: el ahorrar dinero." (Translation: "Throughout the years, I've developed only one habit: saving money.") The money he's been saving all those years is already assigned, in his testament, for his children.

Dad – in his days as an "engineer."

Homero Hinojosa did odd jobs for many years, but he never started his "habit" until he got to Detroit, Michigan, where he proudly worked in two industries. In one, he was an Events and Daily Operations Engineer at a hotel – okay, he was a janitor. In the other, he was a Culinary Implements Expert, or a dishwasher. At any rate, it was at the hotel where he was introduced to a notion, which he then put into continuous motion, and it subsequently became a habit that changed his life and the lives of his children, and this habit continues even as I write this book.

You see, in the early 60s, my father's efforts at a Detroit hotel earned him recurrent cash tips from patrons and guests, especially from Major League Baseball's Tigers, who frequented the establishment. Dad tells me, "No me daban propinas por bonito. Me las daban por mi buen servicio." (Translation: "They didn't give me tips because I was pretty. They gave them to me because of my great service.") He says he worked hard at being *of service*.

These tips, this sudden cash in my dad's pockets and in the pockets of the rest of the custodians, naturally led to excitement, which then ignited action. *Let's do something with this money,* they thought. And so it was that during rest periods at the hotel, most everyone from the Janitorial Department would gather around a table and play card games for money. My father and another co-worker were the only ones who did not participate. In fact, this co-worker was the foreman, and he probably gave dad the best tip of all; he is credited with showing dad the difference between *sight* and *insight*. As regards to sight, my father plainly saw most of the men gamble away their limited cash. Insight, on the other hand, was a totally different concept for him. He could now see with much more clarity – and he had his colleague to thank for that. Dad was advised not to gamble and risk losing all his money. Instead, he should put it in a savings account at the bank.

It turns out that the bank was across the street, and every time my dad's tips reached the five-dollar mark, he went to the bank and made a deposit. Sometimes, he literally crossed the street up to four times a day! My dad was now a changed man. Darren Hardy put it nicely when he said, "When you look at a situation with a different set of eyes, it appears that the situation has changed, though it is *you* who has changed." How true.

To my father and The Buffetts, winning is a habit – an acquired behavior they have mastered until it has become instinctive, like a knee-jerk reflex. They have also diversified; they have kept a reserve; they have put away something for a rainy day...or for a hurricane, like Katrina. Homero Hinojosa and Warren Buffett are habitual winners and financial geniuses that are in the habit of speaking... **The Language of Winners!**

Chapter 9

INSULTS –

A man's own good breeding is the best security against other people's ill manners.

~ Lord Chesterfield

Insults [in-suhlts] *Origin*: 1560–70; < Latin *insultāre* to jump on, insult, equivalent to *in-* in-²+ -*sultāre*, combining form of *saltāre* to jump; see saltant.[69]

Saltant [sal-tnt] *Origin*: 1595–1605; < Latin *saltant-* (stem of *saltāns,* present participle of *saltāre* to jump about, dance, frequentative of *salīre* to jump), equivalent to *sal-* jump + -*t-* frequentative suffix + -*ant-* -ant.[70]

– • –

ONE AFTERNOON, MY WIFE AND I ATTENDED our daughter's high school track meet. As we headed to a spot where we could have a better view, we walked by one of my college students in the stands. Naturally, I went up to him, greeted him, and shook his hand – and the hands of the other people sitting with him. The next day in class, my student (in his early 30s) made it a point to say the following in front of the rest of the class (mainly 20-22 year olds): "Sir, after you shook our hands yesterday, my Dad asked me who you were. I said, *'That's my karate instructor'* and he said, *'Karate? Ka-ra-te? He doesn't look like much!'* " My student proceeded to laugh aloud after he said this, perhaps expecting an army of embarrassment to march in. It did not.

Never missing a great opportunity to teach a valuable lesson, I said instead, "Perfect! That's the best thing your Dad could have told you about me! That's ab-so-lute-ly perfect!" Of course, my student's jaw dropped because this is not the way this whole scene was supposed to play out. Adults with open mouths don't look like they are bursting with confidence.

I continued, "You see, class, whenever you don't look like much… you don't threaten anyone. And because you are not an imposing figure, then others will take you for granted. They won't account for you. They'll underestimate you. They won't be prepared when you –"

KIAI!

I quickly and powerfully unleashed an earth-shattering yell while I punched at an imaginary opponent. Time stood still. The only movements I noticed from my students were faint:

eyes enlarged, pupils dilated, and saliva was swallowed in slow motion.

"The element of surprise is one of your most valuable weapons," I said. "So, never underestimate anyone – because the next time you see someone who *doesn't look like much*, that person could be your next karate instructor, your next boss, or even the person who saves your life."

We then proceeded with our kicking drills. But things would never be the same after that day. My students were now engaged! They showed noticeable, global improvements, from better listening skills to sharper techniques with more *Umph!* As always, I was privileged to guide their personal growth, humbled by their dedication, and glad I was part of the journey.

Winners are comfortable in their own skin; they do not need to pretend to be someone else; they are relaxed, confident, and unaffected by naysayers. Being comfortable in your own skin means that you do not need to have "thick skin" in order to do well in certain business models. The adage goes something like this: *If you want to succeed in this business, you have to have thick skin.* Of course, the reference is that if your skin is thick, it is impenetrable and objections, insults, negativity, and rejection cannot adversely affect you. More often than not, I've heard this adage as it applies to sales and marketing.

Visualize bullets ricocheting off your rough and tough skin, arrows breaking on impact, and an army of *No's* retreating in defeat. That's all fine and good, but what about the additional image of thick, dry, scaly, cracked, and fissured skin? I do not believe an elephant is very comfortable in this skin; it's certainly not a pretty picture. Now, instead of that, picture yourself with soft, smooth, healthy, and vibrant skin. Does this sound like the skin you'd rather have?

So, why not improve the axiom and say "To succeed in this business, you need to have soft, silky, smooth skin!" And now, the reference is still that your skin will be impenetrable to all the negativity because it will simply *slide off* your body without any untoward effects. Winners do not refer to themselves as having thick, unhealthy skin; they choose healthy, vibrant skin.

Let's now observe how the proper use of language can stop verbal bullying in its tracks. President Lincoln recounted a dream in which he found himself at a large assembly. In the dream, as the Red Sea of people parted to let him through, he heard someone say, "He is a common-looking fellow." Lincoln stopped, turned to the man, and calmly said, "Friend, the Lord prefers common-looking people – that is the reason he made so many of them."[71]

True, Lincoln was anything but eye candy. Many believed he was afflicted with Marfan's Syndrome or another skeletal system abnormality. He was tall and lanky, and seemed malnourished – but there was nothing wrong with his brain. In fact, he was a self-taught master of language, and his elocution, cognition, and quick wits about him (apparently, even in his dreams) allowed him to command respect and admiration.

Insults, however, are not restricted to the verbal realm. They can, and many times do, escalate to physical attacks. Our responsibility, as winners, is to avoid physical confrontations at all costs and to realize that combat should only be considered as a last resort. The collateral damages and the long-term ramifications can be devastating, both legally and personally.

American newscaster, David Brinkley had this to say about physical attacks: *A successful man is one who can lay a firm foundation with the bricks others have thrown at him.* As a freshman at Brown University, a strong foundation was indeed laid, as I was frequently "tested" with insults, racial remarks, and physical challenges to fight. That's right, in an Ivy League institution where, supposedly, the students were more...cultured! I guess that at 5'10" and 145 lbs, I was not thought of as a worthy opponent. I, however, avoided as many fights as I could – although a few slipped through the cracks.

One evening, a hulk – you know the type, someone who is so muscular that he can't turn his head without turning his whole body – wearing a muscle shirt came to my dormitory room at Bronson House unannounced. We had never met, but apparently he had heard about me; he had heard that a Mexican kid was pretty good at that karate stuff. In actuality, that year (1976) was the very first time I had been introduced to the martial arts, and as the Treasurer of the Brown Karate Club (and later, President), I took my involvement in the martial arts very seriously. So, this muscle-bound guy just shows up and says, "Let's fight!" and he put up his dukes.[72] Being quick on my feet, I said, "Sure, I'll fight you!" And since he thought we were good to go, he started to jump around. I immediately put up my hand in a halting motion and said, "I'll fight you *if*..."

"If you can beat me at pushups," I said. He was very obedient and promptly went down on all fours. As he was about to begin, I stopped him. "Ah, ah, ah," I said, shaking my index finger at him, "...not like that." He was puzzled. I pointed to my clenched fist and added, "On your knuckles!"

As I said, he was very obedient, and he quickly started doing one pushup after another on his knuckles. After about ten pushups, he began to struggle...but he continued, for he was on a mission. Let me add that he did not breathe once during this whole ordeal. At about sixteen, his arms were trembling and his face was red as a beet. He collapsed after twenty, managing to save his face from exploding. His knuckles, on the other hand, could not be saved; at least four of them were bleeding freely. Did I forget to mention that our competition was taking place on a rough, concrete floor? Anyway, he was huffing and puffing, as he waited for me to do my pushups.

I went to the floor and in machine-gun rhythm, I matched his twenty in no time. Never stopping, number twenty-one was done in super slow motion in order to accentuate my win. I got up victorious and his entire body shook uncontrollably for a few seconds before he stormed off like a paper tiger,[73] never to be heard from again. I had succeeded in beating him without ever having to throw a punch!

Two years later, I saw *Enter the Dragon* for the very first time. If you are a Bruce Lee fan, you know that this is his most famous film and that it was released after Bruce's untimely death in 1973. In the film, there is a scene where several competitors are being taken by boat to a secret island to compete in a global martial arts tournament. Bruce's character, appropriately named Mr. Lee, is on that boat and so is a bully who has been making his rounds on board. The bully spots Mr. Lee and starts to punch toward him, to intimidate him. Since Mr. Lee is comfortable in his own skin and he is not bothered at all, the bully asks, "What's your style?" Mr. Lee answers calmly, "I call it the art of fighting without fighting." Obviously, the bully has never heard of this, so he says, "Show me." Mr. Lee agrees but they are going to have to take a smaller boat and get to a nearby island so he can fight him with his new style. So, when the bully climbs on the smaller vessel to row to the island to fight, Bruce gives the anchoring rope to all the bully's prior victims so they can get back at their aggressor. In essence, Mr. Lee defeated his opponent without having to physically fight him.

Brain over brawn will lead to many victories. My good friend, undefeated world champion Eric Lee (no relation to Bruce), loves to reminisce about the good 'ole days when he competed. Actually, I'm the one who loves to pick his brain about the 100+ world championships that he won. At any rate, he says that many martial artists would try to "psyche him out" prior to the competition by posturing and by invading his personal space. They would perform intricate techniques right in front of him, as he stretched on the floor.[74] One day, one of these alpha males demanded, "How do you like my technique?" Eric pretended to be consumed by other, more pressing things and after a beat, he finally said, "Oh, you're the one doing all those fancy kicks... you didn't look so good." The intruder was so annoyed by Eric's comments, that he foamed at the mouth[75] during competition and totally forgot what he was supposed to do! By the way, Eric Lee went on to win the division...again.

Now, going from personal-space intruders to physical-space intruders, let's see how the great Mark Twain responded to a home burglary one evening in 1908 as he slept upstairs. The burglars, by the way, were later caught with silverware they had stolen from his home. And, being a prolific man of words, Mr. Twain affixed the following message to his front door:[76]

> *NOTICE.*
> *To the next Burglar.*
>
> *There is nothing but plated ware in this house, now and henceforth. You will find it in that brass thing in the dining-room over in the corner by the basket of kittens. If you want the basket, put the kittens in the brass thing. Do not make a noise — it disturbs the family. You will find rubbers (shoes) in the front hall, by that thing which has the umbrellas in it, chiffonier, I think they call it, or pergola, or something like that. Please close the door when you go away! Very truly yours, S.L. Clemens*

Not everyone who throws "bricks" at you is a bad person – he may simply be insecure, jealous, or afraid. Most people are afraid of the unknown, of what is beyond their imagination, of what is slightly out of reach, of new and innovative ideas, of change! A lot of people are stuck in a rut; they have grown into complacency and stagnation.

And then there are those who are scared to death of success! In her book *A Return to Love*, Marianne Williamson says:[77]

> *Our deepest fear is not that we are inadequate. Our deepest fear is that we are powerful beyond measure. It is our light, not our darkness that most frightens us. We ask ourselves, Who am I to be brilliant, gorgeous, talented, fabulous? Actually, who are you not to be? You are a child of God. Your playing small does not serve the world. There is nothing enlightened about shrinking so that other people won't feel insecure around you. We are all meant to shine, as children do. We were born to make manifest the glory of God that is within us. It's not just in some of us; it's in everyone. And as we let our own light shine, we unconsciously give other people permission to do the same. As we are liberated from our own fear, our presence automatically liberates others.*

Once you come to the realization that you were meant for greatness, you will have removed a huge weight from your shoulders. You will be lighter on your feet; you will find the courage to start a new venture, to go on a trip you had always put off, to begin your self-improvement quest, to live the way you were meant to live.

My good friend Presley Swagerty is a great example of someone who is living the greatness he is meant to live. And when talking about bad people, insults, and negativity, he says,

"To be successful, you have to lie, cheat, and steal!" Wow – talk about bad influences! A lot of people do a double take when he says this, but then he expounds on it, turns it around and makes it positive, and gets everyone to laugh and clap in approval.

An adaptation of Presley's phrase is:

> *To be successful, you have to lie, cheat, and steal! That's right, you have to **lie**... in bed reflecting on all the great information you read today in The Language of Winners! You have to **cheat**... a few minutes out of your busy day so you can read a few more pages of The Language of Winners! And you have to **steal**... a great idea or two from The Language of Winners! and use it to positively impact the lives of others today... and every day!*

Winners transform negatives into positives; insults, critiques, objections, and rejection do not hurt them because they do not take it personal. Winners master the art of fighting without fighting by outsmarting the competition. Winners can turn condescension 180 degrees, from disdain to respect, by simply being proficient in the use of words and language. Winners overcome their fears and quickly come to the realization that they are meant for greatness, power, and success beyond measure. Winners will lie, cheat, and steal – in a good way – to achieve their dreams. Winners lay a solid foundation for success out of all the bricks, insults, and attacks others have hurled at them throughout the years. And you, as a winner, will find that once you are able to turn insults into compliments, you will have mastered a better language – ***The Language of Winners!***

Chapter 10

JUST RIGHT –

Collect as precious pearls the words of the wise and virtuous.
~ Abdel Kader

Just [juhst] *Origin*: 1325–75; Middle English < Latin *jūstus* righteous, equivalent to *jūs* law, right + *-tus* adj. suffix.[78]

Right [rahyt] *Origin*: before 900; (noun and adj.) Middle English; Old English *reht, riht;* cognate with Dutch, German *recht,* Old Norse *rēttr,* Gothic *raihts;* akin to Latin *rēctus,* Old Irish *recht* law, Greek *orektós* upright.[79]

- • -

HOW WOULD IT SOUND if Heinz told you they had "over 50 varieties!" Strange, right? Strange and vague. We all know Heinz has *exactly* 57 varieties. And how would Ivory soap sound if it claimed it was 100% pure! What about Taster's Choice coffee claiming to be 100% caffeine free! Nobody would believe it.

In the March 2009 *SUCCESS CD*, Roger Dawson talks about power negotiating and the importance of using specific numbers. He says, "Specific numbers have credibility. People tend to believe specific numbers, but they'll counter propose on rounded numbers."[80] That's why Taster's Choice coffee is 99.7% caffeine free and Ivory soap is 99.44% pure. Wow, those are very specific numbers – the soap down to the one-hundredths of a point. This number must have come from a research laboratory, so it's got to be true! And since people tend to believe detailed information rather than broad, generalized statements, does it make sense, then, to strive to use *exact figures* when referring to numbers? Of course, it does.

Not only are you more credible, but the numbers you quote may mean the difference between a new business associate joining your team or not, a potential customer buying from you or not, a patient deciding to switch doctors or not, or even the difference between life and death!

First, let's look at a business example: Say you have been invited to attend a presentation at the conference room in a local hotel. The speaker is charismatic, he has good stage presence, and he enunciates clearly and projects his voice all the way to the back of the room. There is positive energy in the venue and so far, you are excited about the opportunity to learn more about this company.

Then, he gets to the numbers. He presents the figures for your expected customer base in this business and says, "Over two-thousand customers." Well, this bothers you. It bothers you because you don't know if it is two-thousand one-hundred twenty-five or five-thousand two-hundred fifty... but you let it go.

Then he gets to the compensation plan and says that you will be earning "over $7,000 a month!" Again, this nags at you. It nags at you because it's *your income* he is not clear about. And now, you are really starting to doubt this wonderful presenter, this wonderful business opportunity, and this wonderful company.

Why can't he tell you your exact salary? Why can't he give you specific numbers? Is he hiding something? In the end, you do not feel you can trust someone who rounds-off important numbers like you just heard. And although it wasn't an incapacitating pain, this thorn on your foot pestered you enough to the point that you hobbled away from this opportunity. If this had been a TV show (say, *Dragnet*), then you would have been Sergeant Joe Friday saying, "Just the facts, ma'am. Just the facts."

So, now you have a foot problem and you've hobbled all the way to your Podiatrist – he promptly excises the thorn and your foot is fine now. The following week, you find yourself in your Family Doctor's office, anxiously awaiting your lab results from two weeks ago. You have not been able to sleep well since your blood was drawn, and today is the day when you will get some answers. The waiting room is standing room only, and you have taken off from work early so that you could come for this important appointment.

After a nerve-wracking 45 minutes in the lobby, you are taken to the nurse's station, where you remove your shoes and other items that add extra weight to your total. Already, you do not feel good because you are nervous, it is taking a long time for this, and now you have also gained some weight, which gets documented along with your higher-than-usual blood pressure. Next, you sit in the examination room for another 25 minutes, at which point the Physician's Assistant finally walks in. She informs you that the Doctor is at the hospital in an emergency, and asks if it is okay that she reviews your laboratory results with you. Although you would rather not, you answer in the affirmative and here is a hypothetical scenario of what happens next:

PA: Good news – your *Homocysteine* level is below 10!

You: Uh, *below* ten?

PA: Yes, less than 10 is what the Doctor recommends.

You: Well, yes – but only *if* there are no other risk factors for heart disease. And I have risk factors, as you can see from my chart. That's why he wanted my results to be less than 7.2.

PA: Oh, I wasn't aware...

You: So, what's my result?

PA: *(shuffles through chart)* Uh, you're at 9.8.

You: *(mumbles)* How's that good news?

PA: I'm sorry?

You: The Doctor said if I wasn't below 7.2 he was going to recommend I go to the Cardiologist for a "catheter" or something.

PA: A *catheterization*. And the Cardiologist would have to decide that.

You: Yes, and *I* have to decide if I want to continue coming here.

PA: Why do you say that?

You: Because you obviously don't know what's going on.

PA: Uh...

You: Maybe I'll come back later, when the Doctor can see me.

In this scenario, the lack of an exact number was the last straw. It pushed the patient over the edge; the patient ran out of patience – and an impatient patient is not a good thing.

There had been two long weeks of waiting and insomnia, followed by a crowded waiting room and more waiting, and then the unusually high blood pressure reading and a few more pounds added to an already at-risk individual. Finally, the trusted person was not available and the substitute did not take the time and/or did not know better, setting up an unfortunate outcome.

Thus, when it comes to numbers, paying attention to detail can be extremely important. I am reminded of the story of the penny that doubles every day for a month. I had heard this story a while back and it had not resonated like it did when Darren Hardy spoke to me in his audio book, *The Compound Effect*.[81]

Naturally, I tried it out on my own "laboratory" – my karate class. I asked them, "Class, if I were to give you one million dollars cash right now, or a penny that doubles in value every day for a month, which would you take?" I would say "a month" instead of "thirty-one days," to be vague and to minimize the importance of thirty-one days versus thirty days. Naturally, most of my students answered, "the one million bucks." Occasionally, I would have a few students go against convention and thus, choose the penny. But when I asked why the penny, they would say something like, "Because it's a trick question," or "Because it's more?" They would pose it as a question, not as a statement. So, they were not sure.

Invariably, they were shocked when they found out it was more than ten million dollars! However, they were more in awe when I would recite, "After thirty-one days, the penny is now ten million, seven-hundred-thirty-seven thousand, four-hundred eighteen dollars and twenty-four cents!" And because I said it with such confidence and conviction – and, most importantly, because it is a very *specific* number – they believed me! None of my students questioned the accuracy of this number during class. I challenged them to double check it at home with their calculators, and I am sure some did.

I told this story about my karate class to one of my business partners and good friend, Freddy Peralta. Freddy is an eloquent Spanish public speaker and businessman, and he thought it was a great story so he incorporated it into his speech about a year later. When he got to the accrued amount after thirty-one days, he could not remember the exact numbers – he just remembered, like most, that it totaled to more than ten million dollars. So, he decided to put me on the spot and asked with a smirk, "Doctor Hinojosa, what was that amount?" To everyone's surprise, including mine, I confidently stated the figure of $10,737,418.24! Freddy showed his pearly whites and added, "After all this time, I never thought you'd remember all the numbers!" And after Freddy's presentation, I was a celebrity of sorts. Several business prospects approached me with big smiles, and everyone was better for it.

It is often said that "money talks," but I believe that the exact amount of money communicates "just right" – the correct amount of money talks in a more *persuasive* fashion. That is why completely accurate numbers clearly enunciate... **The Language of Winners!**

Chapter 11

KINETICS –

Action is the foundational key to all success.
～ Pablo Picasso

Kinetics [ki-net-iks, kahy-] *Origin*: 1850–55; < Greek *kīnētikós* moving, equivalent to *kīnē-* (verbid stem of *kīneîn* to move) + *-tikos* –tic.[82]

- • -

THE HUMAN BODY WAS MADE FOR MOVEMENT; it is an inherently kinetic masterpiece. Why else then, would we have hundreds of joints? Let's face it, if we were designed for inactivity, the number of joints in the human body would eventually wither away to the single digits. So, if we are innately kinetic, why is it that many of us spend much of our time idle – idle in our physical conditioning, idle in our personal improvement, idle in our imagination and creativity, idle in our dreams and aspirations, idle in our relationships, and idle in planning for a better future?

The Kinesiology Department at South Texas College in McAllen, Texas was also idle to a certain degree in the early part of this millennium. Kinesiology, as you know, is the study of motion, especially as it pertains to the human body. In 2003, I accepted a faculty position as the Karate instructor for the college – all Kinesiology majors were required to take two semesters with me. I spent a number of truly enjoyable years there and I hope to return to the college to continue teaching someday.

Often, I would ask my class if they agreed with the adage, "Knowledge is power." Invariably, everyone nodded in agreement, but then I would say, "What good does it do if I *know* what technique I must execute to defend myself during a crisis, and I don't carry it out?" I would then add, "Knowledge *plus action* is power!"

And I would perform a take-down when I said the word "action," all the while, making sure I did not hurt the student on the way down. Or I would throw a reverse punch to another student's solar plexus, barely tapping him so he would still experience the impact, while I simultaneously belted out an earth-shattering *Kiai!*, completely immobilizing him due to the shock of the sudden yell. Needless to say, the Karate class at South Texas College was always entertaining and fun.

Thus, the action step seems to be the catalyst for most success formulas. For instance, many successful individuals recite something to the tune of, "Luck is when preparation meets opportunity." Yes, you have to prepare – study, read, learn, practice, exercise, memorize, and whatever else you must do to get ready. Then, when the opportunity finally arrives, you are able to recognize it and you can take advantage of it to maximize your results. And that is how your fortune will improve – it will improve, that is, only if you take action! Once again, what good is it if you are prepared when opportunity comes knocking *and* you don't do anything about it! Therefore, I believe the new formula should look something like this:

Preparation + Opportunity + Action = Luck!

Likewise, the action you perform must be aligned with your goals; the action must take you closer to what you are trying to accomplish. Benjamin Franklin reminds us to "never confuse motion with action." For example, let us take the first enhanced proverb from this chapter: *Knowledge plus action is power!*

Say, you are being robbed at gunpoint and you have the knowledge, you have the perfect defense against this particular attack. However, instead of executing the counter-technique that will save your life, you start dancing the twist! That move is certainly not getting you closer to your goal; it is getting you closer to your attacker's goal! Unless, of course, you are doing it as a distraction that will be followed by a more definitive move a split second later.

The same applies for my belief that "Luck is when preparation meets opportunity... and you take action." Let's say, you have been studying and learning your company's business presentation and you want to be the presenter at the next meeting. You have already fulfilled the minimum requirements to be a presenter, but your supervisor has not given you the green light yet; he has other people in mind. Then, at the meeting, your supervisor taps you on the shoulder and asks that you be the presenter for the event because the scheduled presenter is running late and the company cannot afford to wait any longer. You have been preparing yourself for this opportunity and now it's time for you to shine and get lucky, right? Right – unless you run in the other direction screaming at the top of your lungs! Running away screaming is not action directed at attaining your goal; it is action directed at getting you fired! Instead of the good fortune that this equation promotes, you have just created a bit of bad fortune for yourself.

Motivational guru, Tony Robbins, says that "the path to success is to take massive, determined action." I agree – the determined action he is referring to is the focused, directed, indomitable action that will take you closer to your goals, instead of farther away from them.

Personal development leaders remind us that in order to succeed, you must have visibly thought out plans that you organize and work on every day. The maxim comes to mind, "plan your work and work your plan." Once more, the operative word here (i.e., the verb "work") refers to action that is directed and focused at a clearly defined goal. On the other hand, the "plan" you are working is the roadmap you have designed for your success, the roadmap for you to get from point A to point B. "A genius without a roadmap will get lost in any country; an average person with a good roadmap will go straight and true to their destination," says Brian Tracy.

James R. Sherman, PhD, in his book *Plan Your Work / Work Your Plan*, says that "Planning is the design of a hoped-for future and the development of effective steps for bringing it about." He says that planning "helps you identify the *hazards* and *opportunities* that can determine your chances of success."[83] He is referring to the roadmap for success. He could very well be saying, "Planning is the roadmap for a better future and the development of *action steps* and strategies for making it a reality." As is the theme of this chapter, action will get you there. What good is a great roadmap for a better tomorrow if you never take that first step? You have to start moving in the direction of your dreams.

Yes, plan your work – but do not spend all your time on the planning stage at the expense of the action stage. Some people avoid this "action" because they are afraid of what may happen once they begin the heavy lifting; they are afraid of objections or, even worse, rejection; they are scared to death of what others may think of them.

Sure, if you never ask for the sale you will never get a *No*... but you will also never get anywhere in your business. So, enough already; start trekking and work your plan! And, as Confucius said, "When it is obvious that the goals cannot be reached, don't adjust the goals, adjust the action steps." Work differently; work smarter, not harder; but get to work.

Winners have clearly defined goals and action plans to get them there; they plan their work and work their plan; they follow a great roadmap on their journey toward success. Winners work, work, work, consistently – that is why they accomplish all that they do – and when they cannot reach their goals, they simply modify their activity in order to succeed. Winners understand that without action, nothing gets done. Action is the catalyst for success; action is focused, incessant movement to reach a goal; action is the common denominator seen in winners who articulate... **The Language of Winners!**

Chapter 12

LEADERSHIP –

The ultimate measure of a man is not where he stands in moments of comfort, but where he stands at times of challenge and controversy.
~ Martin Luther King, Jr.

Leadership [lee-der-ship] *Origin*: before 900; Middle English *leden*, Old English *lædan* (causative of *līthan* to go, travel); cognate with Dutch *leiden*, German *leiten*, Old Norse *leitha*, -er + -ship Middle English, Old English -*scipe;* akin to shape; cognate with dialectal Frisian, dialectal Dutch *schip*.[84]

Lead [leed] *Origin*: "to guide," O.E. lædan "cause to go with one, lead," causative of liðan "to travel," from W.Gmc. *laithjan (cf. O.S. lithan, O.N. liða "to go," O.H.G. ga-lidan "to travel," Goth. ga-leiþan "to go"). Meaning "to be in first place" is from late 14c. The noun is first recorded c.1300, "action of leading." Meaning "the front or leading place" is from 1560s.[85]

- • -

A TYPICAL "CALL TO ACTION" CLOSE I've heard a multitude of times in business meetings goes like this:

> *Ladies and gentlemen, there are three kinds of people in this world – those who* make *things happen, those who stand on the sidelines and* watch *things happen, and those who stand around and say 'what in the world just happened?' Which one are you? We hope you're a go-getter that makes things happen, because we want you on our team. Thank you for your time! We'll stick around to answer any of your questions, and to welcome you to the team!*

First of all, the go-getter in this example has all the desirable attributes, like leadership qualities, enthusiasm, vitality, influence, and a positive attitude. Everyone in the audience would like to be thought of as being this success-minded. Likewise, having these attributes indicates that you should commit to joining the team because that's who they are looking for.

Next, those who watch things happen are people who are afraid of taking risks; they have difficulties making decisions; they are simply not motivated nor convinced; they may suffer from one of a number of medical maladies, such as *Paralysis by Analysis,* whereby they are too busy finding out everything there is to know about the topic, that they are paralyzed into inactivity; or they lack the drive, desire, and determination to go after their dreams and make them a reality. If this type of individual sounds like you, the insinuation is that you are not really pursuing your purpose in life; you are not fulfilling your true potential. As the great Jim Rohn says, "Our ultimate life objective should be to create as much as our talent and ability and desire will permit. To settle for doing less than we could do is to fail in this worthiest of undertakings." And maybe, just maybe, you will start agreeing with his philosophy and realize that "for things to change in your life, **you** have to change!" So, are you ready to join the team?

And finally, the third kind of person is the worst because he has no clue. He did not know what just hit him. He has been shown a life-altering opportunity for himself and his family, perhaps for generations to come, and he cannot see it. This description alludes to an undesirable I.Q. and nobody in the audience wants to think he is not smart enough. This person may be lured into joining the team just because he doesn't want to appear stupid.

Once again, in one of his many teachings, Jim Rohn shares with us *How to Avoid Being Broke and Stupid*.[86] He says that in order for you not to be broke, don't be stupid. In other words, you are stupid if you do not team up with successful individuals such as the ones you have just heard. You are stupid if you do not continue reading and learning everything you can to improve yourself. And if you learn from these successful individuals and you put into practice what you have learned, then you won't be broke anymore.

So, the message on the third kind of person is that if you do not join this team, you will still be broke...and now you are also stupid. And Jim Rohn says there is nothing worse than that, unless you are sick too – then you will be sick, broke, *and* stupid. But, if you are unfortunate enough to also be ugly, then that's as low as you can get, because now you are ugly, sick, broke, *and* stupid.[87] Nobody wants to be in this category, so join the team and start improving your life now!

Hence, you have decided you do not want to belong to the latter category – you would rather be part of the go-getters, the leaders. But how do you *become* a leader? Great question – leadership is an ongoing process. You don't just wake up one day and announce to the world, "I am a leader!" and you don't suddenly yell at the top of your lungs, "Follow me – I shall lead you!" Jeff Olson, in his audio book *The Slight Edge*, says that continuous study, then action, followed by modeling an expert in the field, and incessantly repeating this process will one day make you worthy of emulating. You will thus, transform into a leader through diligently "pursuing the path of self-mastery and continuous learning."[88]

John C. Maxwell also believes that there has to be continuous learning...even *within* the different leadership levels, of which he says there are five. Maxwell has taught for more than 30 years the five levels of leadership, which are, from lowest to highest: Position, Permission, Production, People Development, and Pinnacle.[89]

As a *positional* leader, people follow you because they have to – you are the boss. In the *permission* level, people follow you because they want to – you have established, and are now developing, relationships. As a leader in the *production* level, you are getting results and people follow you because of what you have done for the organization. The *people development* level is a reproduction level – people follow you because of what you have done for them; this is where massive growth can occur. And lastly, the highest level of leadership is the *pinnacle* level, where you have garnered universal respect – people follow you because of who you have become and what you represent.[90]

A case study of a significant person who *makes things happen* can be found in the October 2010 issue of *SUCCESS* magazine. In this issue's *SUCCESS* CD, John Maxwell reads about Dr. William Foege, a world-renowned physician who worked on the successful campaign to eradicate smallpox. Maxwell highlights Foege's global health achievements in order to exemplify the five qualities of individuals who make things happen. Maxwell says that people who make things happen: 1) are driven for a cause, 2) feel their work is a calling, 3) do not have an easy path, 4) think outside the box, and 5) do more than is required or expected. At the end of the segment, Maxwell goes on to list the seven things that make leaders effective:[91]

1) *Do I set direction and cast vision well?*
2) *Do I cultivate a culture of growth?*
3) *Do I achieve results with others?*
4) *Do I engage and develop a consensus with others?*
5) *Do I lead well in a crisis?*
6) *Do I recreate myself and my organization when needed?*
7) *Do I make things happen?*

Essentially, Maxwell says that people who make things happen are driven by a power greater than themselves; they are passionate about what they are doing; they have had to overcome difficult challenges; they have had to be creative and innovative; and they have gone the extra mile. And they do all these things willingly! If this seems like a lot of hard work, it is... for someone who does not have their passion, their drive, their creativity, and their work ethic. On the other hand, for individuals that make things happen, it is a joy to do what they do. It is not work – it is living the life they chose and in the process, they are becoming more effective leaders. There is no doubt, people who *make things happen* speak loud and clear because they speak... ***The Language of Winners!***

Chapter 13

Mannerisms –

Personality is an unbroken series of successful gestures.
~ F. Scott Fitzgerald

Mannerisms [man-uh-riz-uhms] *Origin*: 1125–75; Middle English *manere* < Anglo-French; Old French *maniere* Vulgar Latin **manuāria,* noun use of feminine of *manuārius* handy, convenient (Latin: of, pertaining to the hand). See manus, -er -isms < Greek *-ismos, -isma* noun suffixes, often directly, often through Latin *-ismus, -isma,* sometimes through French *-isme,* German *-ismus* (all ultimately < Gk).[92]

- • -

IN HIS DISTINCTIVE WAY OF CONVEYING A MESSAGE, the inimitable Jim Rohn articulates the following in the November 2009 *SUCCESS* CD:[93]

Success leaves clues. Watch how the man shakes hands. Watch how the lady responds. People who do well do certain things over and over... and if you're clever, you can pick them up. Watch it all – if a guy is making $10,000 a month, I'd watch how he walks. Maybe that's it! Copy his funny little walk. Somebody says, "Well, that's kind of a silly walk." It's 10,000! I haven't got the money yet, but I've got the walk! It's bound to start somewhere. What I ask you...is to be unusual and be a good observer of what's going on. You can pick up ideas that can change your life starting tomorrow!

That's right, observe what's going on and study the literature. For example, a 2011 University of California, Berkeley, study of non-verbal communication found that people determine within seconds if someone is trustworthy, kind, or compassionate based on a few key factors – namely, how often the subject makes eye contact, smiles, nods while listening, and displays an open body posture.[94] Successful individuals will note that 3 out of the 4 parameters that yield immediate results are facial expressions. Thus, it behooves us to discover a few facial pearls.

For instance, say you simply loved *The Language of Winners!* and you wish to give a friend an autographed copy of the book. (Contact me, I can make it happen!) You notice that upon receiving the book, your friend smiles. But is your friend's smile genuine or not? Well, if the only thing on your friend's face that moves is the lips, you disappointed her. If, however, the smile is accompanied by a crinkling at the corners of the eyes (the so called, *Crow's feet*) and the cheeks raise a bit, you are a hit![95]

Thus, when you observe someone with the dreaded Crow's feet, that is a good sign – despite the fact that many women believe it is a sign of aging for them and a sign of character for men. These changes around the eyes actually imply that you have spent a lot of time sharing legitimate smiles with others! So, don't be too hasty in going to the Plastic Surgeon or getting the *botulinum toxin* injections to try and erase those signs of happiness and fulfillment. They are there for a reason.

Winners use a technique known as "mirroring" to put others at ease.[96] Essentially, you match what the other person is doing in a few key instances, like when you shake hands or when you make eye contact. Upon receiving the other person's hand into yours, quickly determine the strength or gentleness of the interaction and do the same – it will make a good first impression. Likewise, try to reciprocate the eye contact with the other person, being careful not to stare or to look away too soon. By having this balance of eye contact, you are engaging the other person and enhancing your time together. If, on the other hand, someone avoids eye contact, they are really saying: I am not interested in talking to you; I do not like you; I am trying to deceive you; I do not approve; I am not attracted to you.[97]

And because the eyes are the windows to the soul, they allow winners to find out what is really going on inside.[98] For example, dilated pupils mean that the person you are talking to is comfortable and receptive; that individual is happy to see you and does not want to leave anytime soon. The pupils have gotten bigger in order to see more of you, as much as possible; they are permitting more information about you to be processed that very moment. However, do not misinterpret dilated pupils at night – physiologically, the pupils will dilate when the sun sets to allow more light to come in, so you can better interpret what you are seeing.

But in order to determine whether someone's pupils are dilated or not, you have to be in close proximity. On the other hand, when you find yourself far enough away that you are not able to gauge the size of the pupils, it is time to focus your attention at the "bigger picture," such as body posture. Mark Asher, in his book *Body Language*, talks about the importance of posture in the following:[99]

> *Poor posture can signal a lack of self-esteem. A person who is hunched up, head down, eyes to the ground, round shouldered and with splayed feet is hardly likely to galvanize our attention for long. We immediately pick up messages of shame, humility and withdrawal. Conversely, a person who stands up straight and walks tall captures our attention far more. Here is a character displaying an interest in his surroundings and the people around him... Our postures change as we shift weight from one foot to another. Therefore, if we shift backwards and forwards we make ourselves look cunning – giving the impression that we are trying to wriggle out of the situation we find ourselves in.*

Another aspect of posturing is seen in martial arts stances. For instance, the *Attention Stance* in Tae Kwon Do is a position of alertness and heightened awareness.[100] It consists of standing straight with relaxed shoulders; the eyes are alert and look straight ahead; the hands are open and the palms touch the sides; and the feet are together. The full representation of this stance can only be accomplished by a serious martial artist –

one who is serious about his health and personal hygiene, and serious about wearing a clean, pressed uniform.

But proper uniforms and attire are not only important in the martial arts. In fact, people will make assumptions about your wealth, status, and even your health, by assessing your clothes and appearance. Our appearance is meticulously scrutinized by others. Mark Asher declares, "Every physical feature from the size of our chest, the length of our hair, our waistline, even the size of our shirt collar is essentially a non-verbal piece of communication that an observer will sift and sort through, mostly subconsciously..."[101]

Winners take care of their personal appearance. As Jim Rohn used to say, "To attract others, you have to be attractive." Certainly, if you do not exercise, eat right, and get enough restful sleep, your health and your appearance will suffer.

In my medical thriller, *The Tonic*, the following takes place when the tension builds and Alfred Campbell has had enough of John Stone. For these two fictional characters, the scene reaches a boiling point because of appearances:[102]

> " – and for heaven's sakes, Stone," he said as if he'd been talking all along. "Do something about that ugly hair of yours." This wasn't the first time he'd lectured

> Stone about this, nor would it be the last. "What do you do with all your money, anyway?"

Perhaps one of the *easiest* ways to appear more attractive is by wearing something that is free: a smile. After all, "it takes 72 muscles to frown, but only 14 to smile," says Zig Ziglar.[103] However, according to the Chief of Plastic and Reconstructive Surgery at the University of Chicago Hospitals, David H. Song, MD, it takes 12 muscles to achieve a genuine smile, versus 11 muscles to produce a frown.[104] Despite the fact that smiling uses one more muscle than frowning, Dr. Song believes it takes less effort than frowning because people tend to smile more frequently. Thus, the relevant "smile" muscles are in better shape.

Whether your smile muscles are in shape or not, they are extremely important and need to be used more regularly. And to better understand the importance of a smile, here's a wonderful perspective from Rabbi Samson Raphael Hirsch:[105]

> A SMILE costs nothing, but gives much. It enriches those who receive, without making poorer those who give. It takes but a moment, but the memory of it sometimes lasts forever. None is so rich or mighty that he can get along without it, and none is so poor but

that he can be made rich by it. A smile creates happiness in the home, fosters good will in business, and is the countersign of friendship. It brings rest to the weary, cheer to the discouraged, sunshine to the sad, and is nature's best antidote for trouble. Yet it cannot be bought, begged, borrowed, or stolen, for it is something that is of no value to anyone until it is given away. Some people are too tired to give you a smile. Give them one of yours, as none needs a smile so much as he who has no more to give.

Winners understand that success leaves clues, and they will model successful individuals and learn from them every chance they get. Winners realize that a lot of non-verbal cues can be gathered from facial expressions, especially the eyes. Winners will put others at ease by mirroring techniques and open body postures. Winners know the importance of a smile and the fact that it is of no value to anyone until it is given away... and they do, time after time. Ergo, the smile muscles of winners are "in shape!" Winners not only possess fluidity of word and gait, they also dress for success because they believe in the body language of...**The Language of Winners!**

Chapter 14

NETWORK –

The richest people in the world look for, and build, networks; everyone else looks for work.

~ Robert Kiyosaki

Network [net-wurk] *Origin*: before 900; Middle English *net* (noun), net "mesh," from P.Gmc. *natjan (cf. O.N., Du. net, Swed. nät, O.H.G. nezzi, Ger. Netz, Goth. nati "net"), originally "something knotted," from PIE *ned- "to twist, knot" (cf. Skt. nahyati "binds, ties," L. nodus "knot"). O.E. weorc, worc "something done, deed, action, proceeding, business, military fortification," from P.Gmc. *werkan (cf. O.S., O.Fris., Du. werk, O.N. verk, M.Du. warc, O.H.G. werah, Ger. Werk, Goth. gawaurki), from PIE base *werg- "to work" (see urge (v.)).[106]

- • -

THE BIGGER AND STRONGER THE NET, the bigger the fish you can catch. A "big fish" does not only imply size, it also means the fish possesses other desirable attributes. Whether you are fishing out at sea or out in the business market, you want to attract the best that is out there. By networking, you are associating with individuals sharing a common interest; you are providing mutual support and assistance so you can all grow and develop a winning culture... so you can land the big fish.

Networks are composed of large numbers of individuals, each contributing a little bit, everyone pulling in the same direction, and maximizing their results. John D. Rockefeller, America's first billionaire, said, "I would rather earn 1% off 100 people's efforts, than 100% of my own efforts." When you leverage off other people, you are actually working smarter, not harder. That is the beauty of utilizing the powerful net you have built to get the most of what you have at your disposal...people and their connections. That is the philosophy behind Network Marketing companies; they utilize the efforts of many to yield phenomenal results. Many wealthy individuals have attained their fortunes by utilizing this principle.

The old adage, "It's not *what* you know, but *who* you know that matters" supports the importance of building large, strong networks. True, some people have few skills but one or two friends in key positions and that can lead to very bad results with the wrong people ending up in the wrong places. On the other hand, being the proud owner of many skills will not get you up any success ladders if nobody ever finds out about you or what you can bring to the table. There has to be a sense of balance between your skills, talents, abilities, and educational level *and* the people of influence that you have access to, or that you associate with. And when the first part of the axiom is identical between you and a competitor, then *who* you know makes a big difference. As long as integrity and ethics are maintained, *who* you know can positively propel you toward your goals faster than you imagined.

Although the planet's population is increasing, the explosion of technological advances brings credence to the line, "It's a small world, after all." Today, we can instantly connect to someone on the other side of the world. I remember when, as a young boy in 1969, my family huddled around our black and white television set in our small home at 421 Medina Street in Eagle Pass, Texas and watched Neil Armstrong take that "one small step for man; one giant leap for mankind." My aunt, Licha, was visiting from México and she never believed the telecast. She attributed what we were watching to "camera tricks" and many years later, she went to her grave with that same belief. She was a hard-working woman with no formal education who was not able to visualize the vast possibilities available from a dedicated network of individuals, plus technology.

John Guare's 1990 play entitled *Six Degrees of Separation*, then the 1993 film by the same name, includes the following quote by one of the characters:[107]

> *I read somewhere that everybody on this planet is separated by only six other people. Six degrees of separation between us and everyone else on this planet. The President of the United States, a gondolier in Venice, just fill in the names. I find it extremely comforting that we're so close. I also find it like Chinese water torture, that we're so close because you have to find the right six people to make the right connection... I am bound, you are bound, to everyone on this planet by a trail of six people.*

In his book *Outliers*, Malcolm Gladwell writes about the role that opportunities play in one's success. He says that winners "are invariably the beneficiaries of hidden advantages and extraordinary opportunities and cultural legacies that allow them to learn and work hard and make sense of the world in ways others cannot."[108] He goes on to refer to the hiring practices of 1940s and 1950s law firms in New York City by quoting Erwin Smigel's *The Wall Street Lawyer* in the following:[109]

> *...lawyers who are Nordic, have pleasing personalities and "clean-cut" appearances, are graduates of the "right schools," have the "right" social background and experience in the affairs of the world, and are endowed with tremendous stamina. A former law school dean, in discussing the qualities students need to obtain a job, offers a somewhat more realistic picture: "To get a job [students] should be long enough on family connections, long enough on ability or long enough on personality, or a combination of these. Something called acceptability is made up of the sum of its parts. If a man has any of these things, he could get a job. If he has two of them, he can have a choice of jobs; if he has three, he could go anywhere."*

This alludes to the observation that when you are wearing the right attire, the appropriate outfit for the occasion, and more specifically, the right cap – as in, the right <u>c</u>onnections, <u>a</u>bilities, and <u>p</u>ersonality – the doors of possibility will open for you. Yes, doors will open for you, but you still have to work at building and developing a solid network. It is going to take time and a lot of dedicated effort from many individuals – that's why it's called *net-working*, as opposed to *not-working*.

Most people look at simply "building" a network, which entails <u>recruiting, gathering, signing-up, and bringing together your</u>

team. I believe that winners not only *build* a network, they also "develop" their network, which requires training, supporting, nurturing, and guiding them in the right direction – in the direction of the team's vision.

Winners build and develop large, influential networks because they accept the fact that there are only 86,400 seconds in a day and no *one* individual can work more than that in any given day. So, how can winners dedicate more than 86,400 seconds of productive time per day? By bringing others into the network, thus maximizing your efforts and adding *their* time to your totals. Winners understand about leverage and about having a dedicated network of individuals working toward a common goal. Winners work smarter, not harder. The networks of winners snowball and get bigger and bigger until they reach *critical mass*, the point at which your life changes for the better. Winners utilize not only their talents, but also their connections to make noteworthy contributions to society because they *get it* – they get what **The Language of Winners!** is all about.

Chapter 15

OPTIONS –

Why do people arrive at such different places at the end of the journey? Have we not all sailed upon the same sea? The major difference isn't circumstance; it's the set of the sail.

~ Jim Rohn

Options [op-shuhns] *Origin*: c.1600, "action of choosing," from Fr. option, from L. optionem (nom. optio) "choice, free choice," related to optare "to desire, choose," from PIE base *op- "to choose, prefer." Meaning "thing that may be chosen" is attested from 1885. Commercial transaction sense first recorded 1755.[110]

- • -

AS A WINNER, YOUR COMMAND OF LANGUAGE will allow you to have several options at your disposal at all times – options that the average individual will not have because he is not prepared like you are. Say, you are a speaker for your company and tonight you are going to present to a group of potential investors. This is a huge meeting, one that you have been working on for several months, and it is considered the most important meeting in your company's history. No pressure, but at the last minute, your boss lets you know that this group has an aversion to several of the key words within your talk. So, you must adapt quickly and you must choose other words that will still convey your message, and that are just as powerful. In order to accomplish this in such short notice, you must already possess an extensive vocabulary to be able to replace those critical words, those words that will make or break the deal. Can you do it? More importantly, *will* you do it?

My teenage daughter, Laura, went for an interview at a clothing store and she called me afterwards with the follow-up. She was excited to tell me all the details of her interview. At one point, the interviewer said, "Describe what kind of person you are." Laura, without hesitation, responded with one of these two statements:

1. "I'm a very blunt person; I say it like I see it."

2. "I'm an honest person, but tactful."

In both instances, Laura is the same person; the only difference between these two responses is how the interviewer perceives my daughter. Is she caring and thoughtful? Or is she self-centered and conceited?

Leadership expert, John C. Maxwell, describes the difference between *caring* and *candor*.[111] He says that in order for you to be an effective leader, you must attain a balance of both of these options with your team. The fact that you care about someone does not mean you cannot be honest with them; just do it with tact and a keen sense of what is appropriate at that particular moment. That way, you would have avoided offending a teammate, who will now be willing to give more of himself for the greater good, the team. Likewise, my daughter, by being an honest but tactful salesperson, will be better able to deal with delicate situations at the workplace. Thus, caring will get the relationship started, but candor will keep the relationship going.

Care and candor apply for any type of relationship, even a student-teacher relationship. As a junior in high school, Mr. Flores (my Typing teacher) encouraged me to sign up for the University Interscholastic League (U.I.L.) Typing I competition team, the beginner typists. All Typing I competitors qualified by being currently enrolled in the first year of typing and by being in good academic standing. (Today, this class would be called "keyboarding," but since we did not have any computers in those days, it was called "typing.") Every day after school, for three months, we would practice our typing skills and speed. At the end of our very first day of practice, our U.I.L. coach announced to the team that I had already done better than last year's Texas state champion! Everyone was thrilled; we were looking forward to a winning season. Then, it began.

Coach was used to her students faring well in U.I.L., and since I was not enrolled in her class, she wanted me to switch to *her* class. "Anyway," she said, "it's just next door." But I did not want to leave Mr. Flores' class; he was a great teacher and my brother, who was now a senior, was also in the class. To say that I enjoyed Mr. Flores' Typing class would be an understatement. And Coach had two students from her class representing our school, but she wanted me to be her student; I thought we were all her students.

Every day, Coach pleaded with me to switch to her class, and every day I would tell her I was happy with Mr. Flores. I would tell her, "But you're my teacher for U.I.L.!" She was not satisfied; she wanted more. After a few weeks, she finally stopped asking and I felt like a big weight had been removed from my shoulders. Very quickly, my speed improved dramatically and every time Coach returned my practice papers, there was a check mark with the words "Very good!" written next to it. Of course, I saved all my papers.

And so it came; our District competition. Everyone expected me to win, hands down. But I did not; in fact, I didn't even place! And what happened with Coach's two students? They both placed...only to be easily defeated in the next round of competition. They were more than twenty words per minute slower than the fastest representative from our team. So, what happened?

There were certain, specific rules that Coach withheld from me. I was never aware of those rules and, as a consequence, that was the difference maker. You see, we were graded on speed *and* accuracy – even one mistake meant a severe penalty. My paper came back with three mistakes, and nobody wins with three mistakes. I had no clue as to what the judges considered "mistakes." I thought I had done great; I had done like I always did in practice.

At the end of every line, a little bell would ring and you were supposed to press the "return" key. But you could not just press it anywhere, it had to be done within a certain number of spaces, and I was not privy to that information. During every practice for three months, Coach had checked off my papers and added her nice remarks, but she never corrected my deficiencies.

When we returned home from U.I.L., Mr. Flores was shocked to hear that I did not even place. When I showed him all my practice papers and pointed out the many times I could have been corrected, he was furious! Care and candor: I guess Coach cared for me only as long as she believed I may switch to her 6th period class; candor, on the other hand, had been on vacation.

We all have choices. After many years of struggling with this, and although I have not seen her since high school, I opted to forgive Coach. I believe she was misguided; she did not know the set of her sail; she never realized that if *any* of her team won, she won!

But "options" also has to do with the money that winners can generate. True, money cannot buy you love and it cannot buy you happiness, but it can give you options. Money is important because of all the different choices you can make when you have it; and all the limitations you are restricted to, if you do not.

Zig Ziglar says, "Money isn't the most important thing in life, but it's reasonably close to oxygen on the *gotta have it* scale." After only three minutes without oxygen, your brain can suffer serious damage and after four minutes, you risk being declared *brain dead*; certainly, you will not go financially dead after three or four minutes without money, but Zig makes his point the way only he can.

Speaking of the importance of oxygen, one reviewer of my book, *The Tonic*, wrote the following:[112]

> *Adept at using his unique background, Dr. Hinojosa merges his clinical knowledge well into scenes of love,*

> *violence, crime, ethical conflict, emergency-room drama, passion, and more. "Their lips were passionately held together for what seemed like forever," a sentence perhaps used in novels before, is followed by enlightening fresh words: "They were risking hypoxemia, dangerously low levels of oxygen in the blood, as a result of their tightly fastened lips. They were also forgetting to breathe. It was a dangerously wonderful moment for both." Now that's novelty. Have two people ever kissed themselves to death?*

In John Grisham's best-selling novel, *The Testament*, a missionary physician is faced with incredible challenges in the Brazilian jungle due to her lack of money and resources. An attorney from the USA tracks her down to notify her of a large inheritance and tries to convince her to accept the money, which she adamantly refuses. A local girl has just died from a snake bite and the physician says, "...there is an antivenin. I've actually had it here before, and if I'd had it yesterday, the little girl wouldn't have died." The attorney responds by pleading his case: "Then if you had lots of money you could buy lots of antivenin. You could stock your shelves with all the medicines you need. You could buy a nice little outboard to take you to Corumbá and back. You could build a clinic and a church and a school, and spread the Gospel all over the Pantanal."[113] The attorney delineates a lot of specific options applicable to the missionary if money was not an obstacle.

Winners have more options because they are better prepared; they have a more extensive vocabulary, which comes in handy at critical moments. Winners choose to continue studying, practicing, and improving themselves; they care about the person they are becoming. Winners understand that care and candor must co-exist; they understand that doing both consistently and continually will grow a relationship. If someone cares for you, you will accept their brutal honesty, even if it hurts. On the other hand, winners also realize that there is only sorrow in having people be honest with you when you know they really do not care for you.

Winners command more money for their services because of the skills, talents, and overall value they bring to the table. Winners have worked diligently so they can have options in life, so they can make choices others only dream of, and so they can be prepared to recognize and incorporate into their daily lives... ***The Language of Winners!***

Chapter 16

PATIENCE – Part I

It is easier to find men who will volunteer to die, than to find those who are willing to endure pain with patience.

~ Julius Caesar

Patience [pey-shuhns] *Origin*: early 13c., "quality of being patient in suffering," from O.Fr. pacience, from L. patientia "patience, endurance," from patientem (nom. patiens), prp. of pati "to suffer, endure," from PIE base *pei- "to damage, injure, hurt" (see passion).[114]

Passion [pash-uhn] *Origin*: late 12c., "sufferings of Christ on the Cross," from O.Fr. passion, from L.L. passionem (nom. passio) "suffering, enduring," from stem of L. pati "to suffer, endure," from PIE base *pei- "to hurt" (cf. Skt. pijati "reviles, scorns," Gk. pema "suffering, misery, woe," O.E. feond "enemy, devil," Goth. faian "to blame"). Sense extended to sufferings of martyrs, and suffering generally, by early 13c.; meaning "strong emotion, desire" is attested from late 14c., from L.L. use of passio to render Gk. pathos. Replaced O.E. þolung (used in glosses to render L. passio), lit. "suffering," from þolian (v.) "to endure." Sense of "sexual love" first attested 1580s; that of "strong liking, enthusiasm, predilection" is from 1630s. The passion-flower so called from 1630s.[115]

"The name passionflower -- flos passionis -- arose from the supposed resemblance of the corona to the crown of thorns, and of the other parts of the flower to the nails, or wounds, while the five sepals and five petals were taken to symbolize the ten apostles -- Peter ... and Judas ... being left out of the reckoning." ["Encyclopedia Britannica," 1885][116]

- • -

I WAS INTRODUCED TO AMERICA'S PASTIME at the tender age of 8 years, about a year after my family immigrated from México to south Texas. A lot of my classmates understood my ignorance of baseball – they figured I could play soccer, but they were wrong. I had never really taken to sports until I arrived in America.

It was time for Little League and it seemed like the school was electrifying – all the boys were excited! I had no idea what was going on, but the salesman in me took over and I was able to convince my parents to buy me a bat, a glove, and a baseball. I remember the night my dad came home with the essentials – the bat was a shiny dark brown, the baseball was hard as a rock and unblemished, and the glove was simply... stiff. I could not wait to start learning this game, this obsession that had my friends completely spellbound.

The next day when I got home from school, my mother, Rosalinda Fernández de Hinojosa, was busy caring for my four younger sisters – 1 year, 2 years, 3 years, and 5 years of age. My brother, the eldest at 9, was doing his homework. So, my mom took time away from her motherly and *Domestic Engineer* duties and went outside with me. She handed me the bat, showed me the proper hand placement, and gave me a warm, loving smile. Then, she walked five or six paces, turned to face me, and readied herself by hitting the rigid glove twice with the baseball.

Mom – in her days as my baseball "coach."

Mom gave me these words of encouragement as we squared off: "Pégale con todas tus ganas, mi'jo!" (Translation: "Hit it with all your might, son!")

She was in the middle of her wind up when I broke her rhythm with, "Pero, ma', no le quiero pegar a usted." ("But, mom, I don't want to hit you.")

"Ay, mi'jo, no me vas a pegar. Por eso traigo el guante. Ándale, pégale con todas tus ganas." ("Ah, son, you're not going to hit me. That's why I have the glove. C'mon, hit it with all your might.")

Jim Rohn wisely says, "Persistence runs deep like the ocean."[117] And mom was persistent, so I reluctantly gave in and elevated the bat from my right shoulder. Instinctively, I began to shift my weight back and forth, in anticipation of the pitch. Mom started her wind up again, and this time she completed the pitch – an underhanded toss. She, like I, had no idea what we were doing, but she loved learning and engaging with her six kids, just the same.

Like a bell-shaped curve, the hard ball followed its trajectory up and then down. My eyes stayed with it all the way, and as it reached the strike zone at the end of its down slope, I did what any kid with a club in his hand would have done – I swung. And since I was an obedient young boy, I gave it all I had. I believe I even timed the moment of impact perfectly, including my body kinetics, torque, and follow-through. It was awesome! It was a hit! It was a line-drive...right at my mom's shin!

Since she was wearing a dress, I saw the immediate result of the hit – a large black and blue area that covered nearly half of her leg, from the knee down. Mom did not yell, curse, or complain. She simply responded in her usual demeanor; composed, analytical, and in control. She calmly suggested we go inside and look for a piece of raw meat from the fridge. That was my very first baseball practice. One pitcher, one batter, one injury, one make-shift cold pack, and one priceless moment with mom. I was ready for the season. Batter up!

From this introduction to a kids' game, a pastime, a sport, my mother taught me about love, sacrifice, and patience. She was able to bear a painful misfortune to her leg without losing her cool and without complaint.

Those who met my mother did not believe she only went to the 1st grade. She was wise beyond what any formal educational system could offer. She was self-educated and self-motivated, and she inculcated those traits into her children. Also, mom always had a clever adage ready for any situation we faced, and that gave us hope. For example, very early on I learned that I wanted to pursue a career in Medicine, and I was not shy about letting the world know this. But once in a while, when I would get disheartened, when I would get discouraged with my school work, she would encourage me with something like,

"La paciencia es la madre de la ciencia." (Translation: "Patience is the mother of Science.") She knew *what* to say, *when* to say it, and *how* to say it. She spoke like a winner. And that's usually all it took for me to clear my head, shake off the cobwebs, and re-focus.

She would remind me that in today's world, when everyone is in a hurry, when people want things "yesterday," when you can have a drive-by wedding in Las Vegas, when immediate gratification is an entitlement and delayed gratification is obsolete, there is still room for her kids to be the exception...if they just stay – the – course.

Yes, mom taught me about that elusive quality known as patience. As Thomas à Kempis says, "All men commend patience, although few are willing to practice it." I believe those who practice patience can pretty much practice anything else they want.

One of the things that made my mother a winner was her ability to not only pay tribute to the splendor of patience, but also to be one of the rare practitioners of it. Through patience, you can accomplish many things, you can fulfill your dreams, you can conquer the unconquerable, and you can outlast defeat. Winners, like my mother, who develop the attribute of patience, do not get frustrated because they have conquered...***The Language of Winners!***

PATIENCE – Part II

The difference between try and triumph is just a little umph!
~ Marvin Phillips

IN HIS 1840 CLASSIC, *The Teacher's Manual*, Thomas H. Palmer noted that patience and perseverance are not naturally the virtue of youth. That is why he recommended that teachers do their best to excite and promote it by inscribing the following poem somewhere in the classroom where a student's attention could be directed at it in every case of difficulty.[118]

TRY, TRY AGAIN.

'T is a lesson you should heed,
Try, try again;
If at first you don't succeed,
Try, try again;
Then your courage should appear,
For, if you will persevere,
You will conquer, never fear;
Try, try again.

Once, or twice, though you should fail,
Try, try again;
If you would, at last, prevail,
Try, try again;
If we strive, 't is no disgrace,
Though we may not win the race;
What should you do in the case?
Try, try again.

If you find your task is hard,
Try, try again;
Time will bring you your reward,
Try, try again;
All that other folks can do,
Why, with patience, should not you?
Only keep this rule in view,
TRY, TRY AGAIN.

I truly love this poem! It offers time-tested advice regarding the disciplines of patience and perseverance that you can use to motivate your winning efforts. Mr. Palmer prefaced the poem by stating that perseverance is not inherently a virtue of youth – I would venture to say that patience, perseverance, delayed gratification, long-term goal setting, and never giving up are really not virtues of most people in today's world.

In fact, comedy legend W.C. Fields says that, "If at first you don't succeed, try, try again. Then quit. There's no point in being a damn fool about it." I would hope that he was only trying to be funny, because there are countless examples of individuals who persevered despite overwhelming obstacles and repeated failures, only to achieve incredible results.

For instance, Thomas Edison did not succeed in creating the first long-lasting, economically viable, incandescent light bulb after a few attempts. In fact, it is unknown exactly how many times he failed, but it is generally accepted that he made thousands of attempts before achieving his light bulb creation.[119] And when he was asked if he considered himself a failure after so many unsuccessful attempts, he said something to the effect of, "I don't consider myself a failure. I didn't fail 10,000 times; I simply found 10,000 ways that an electric light bulb will not work." Edison was right – that is not failure, that is accumulation of knowledge. And perhaps he was alluding to his multiple challenges with the light bulb when he uttered this quote: "Genius is one percent inspiration, ninety-nine percent perspiration."[120]

Commonly rated as one of America's best Presidents, Abraham Lincoln is another great example of what the virtue of patience can accomplish. Lincoln was the 16th President of the United States, and his personal and professional lives were filled with setbacks and disappointments, one after another. There is even a Lincoln's *Failure List* that has been compiled, chronicling his numerous dejections.[121] Abraham Lincoln proved that even a failure can become President, if he doesn't give up.

These two instances are exceptional illustrations of patience and perseverance, of never giving up, of following through with what you started. But how many people actually stay the course after a few setbacks? In fact, I have seen many people quit after the very first *No*, after the very first rejection. People do not like to be rejected. People want to be liked; people yearn for approval and acceptance. So, if you are a salesperson, the best way to avoid rejection is to either not make any sales calls at all – or if you *do* make a call, then you continue talking and hope that your prospect stops you in mid-sentence and says, "Okay, okay – I'm in!" or "Stop! I'll take it!" or "Where do I sign?" Rejection is tough.

In order to avoid the pain of failure and rejection, some people set the bar so low that they are guaranteed an easy victory. This does not help you grow because you are not challenging yourself. The adage would then be, "If at first you *do* succeed, try a bigger challenge." Darren Hardy tells the story of when, as a young boy, he proudly announced to his father that he didn't fall once at the ski slopes. His father told him that if he didn't fall, it means he didn't get any better. The elder Hardy continued, "If you are going to get better, you have to push yourself. If you push yourself, you are going to fall. Falling is part of getting better."[122] And honestly, there is no shame in falling, the shame lies in you staying down. I always tell my kids, "The harder you fall, the higher you bounce!" On the road to becoming a winner, you will fall, period. The difference between you and everyone else is that for every fall you take, you will get up one more time, *every time* – the way D.J. Gregory does.

On April 4, 2012, ESPN's E:60 program televised a heart-warming story about one man's persistence and his solo pursuit of a dream.[123] The story, entitled "Walk On," shares the struggles of D.J. Gregory, who was born with Cerebral Palsy, underdeveloped lungs, and severely deformed legs. The doctors told the Gregory family, plain and simple, that D.J. would never walk, period.

The Gregory's refused to believe the experts, and D.J. underwent a total of five surgeries on his legs by the time he reached the 1st grade. During his rehabilitations, he advanced from a walker, to two crutches, then one crutch, and finally just a cane. And as he grew, he found he loved sports, but could not play them... except for golf. At the age of 8, he developed a one-arm swing and through lots of patience, sacrifice, and hard work, he came up with a brainstorm as an adult – an idea that would help him stay connected to the sport he loves.

D.J. decided he would walk every hole, of every round, of every tournament during a Professional Golfers' Association (PGA) Tour year – that's over 900 miles! Nobody has ever done that. In reality, that distance is extremely difficult for somebody without any problems in ambulation, let alone for someone who struggles at each step. Finally, at the age of 30, D.J. was allowed to go for his dream; the PGA Tour permitted him to embark on his quest during the 2008 tournament circuit.

During the Tour, D.J. fell multiple times; in fact, he had more than twenty-four falls, but he got up every single time. "It's just another challenge," he said. "I'm gonna fall. That's just the way it is." And when D.J. succeeded in his journey, the voice over announcer exclaimed that this had been "a walk beyond measurement." Yes, D.J. fell many times, but he succeeded when many never even thought he would ever walk.

Failures are merely growth markers on your journey toward success, they are growing pains on your bone lattice of patience, and they are indicators of triumph. And when you try and try and try again, you will triumph because you have just put in a little extra "umph" to your work ethic of perseverance and patience.

In today's Information Technology world, hand-written notes are almost obsolete – people do not have the patience to sit down and write; they would rather click, text, or bang on the keyboard. It is faster, yes, but it is less personable. Well, I believe the following transcribed *hand-written* note by Pixar animator Austin Madison is something more of us should get back to – the hand-written note – for it is truly inspiring:[124]

PIXAR

May 17, 2011

To Whom it May Inspire,

I, like many of you artists out there, constantly shift between two states. The first (and far more preferable of the two) is white-hot, "in the zone" seat-of-the-pants, firing on all cylinders creative mode. This is when you lay your pen down and the ideas pour out like wine from a royal chalice! This happens about 3% of the time.

The other 97% of the time I am in the frustrated, struggling, office-corner-full-of-crumpled-up-paper mode. The important thing is to slog diligently through this quagmire of discouragement and despair. Put on some audio commentary and listen to the stories of professionals who have been making films for decades going through the same slings and arrows of outrageous production problems.

In a word: PERSIST.

PERSIST on telling your story. PERSIST on reaching your audience. PERSIST on staying true to your *vision. Remember what Peter Jackson said, "Pain is temporary. Film is forever." And he of all people should know.*

So next time you hit writer's block, or your computer crashes and you lose an entire night's work because you didn't hit save (always hit save), just remember: you're never far from that next burst of divine creativity. Work through that 97% of murky abysmal mediocrity to get to that 3% which everyone will remember you for!

I guarantee you, the art will be well worth the work! Your friend and mine,
Austin Madison

"ADVENTURE IS OUT THERE!"

At the end of Mr. Madison's hand-written pep talk, he included a drawing of a kid doing the Cub Scout's honor salute. It is a wonderfully inspiring message of persistence from a person who has been there, a person who matters, and a winner – a winner who never quit.

Winners never quit and quitters never win; winners try again and losers never do. The subconscious of winners responds better to "try again" instead of "never quit." Why is that? The words "never quit" are both negative words; "never" and "quit" are filed within the Pessimistic Department of your subconscious and they will harm your psyche and you won't even know what hit you. On the other hand, the words "try again" are filed into your subconscious in the Optimistic Department, where you will get a feeling of renewed energy, you will sense that you have another chance at success, and when there is hope there is always a chance. By using positive, empowering words, you will know exactly why you are feeling uplifted. As a winner, you *choose* to use positive words and positive influences.

In *The Secret Law of Attraction* audio CD, the celebrated Napoleon Hill lists the four (what I call) *Tenets of Perseverance*.[125] I like them so much that I incorporate them into Achievement Certificates whenever I can – as a visual reminder of what it took to get there, and what it will take to continue on the Personal Improvement journey. Here, then, are the Tenets of Perseverance:

1. A definite purpose with a compelling desire for its fulfillment.

2. A definite plan expressed in continuous action.

3. Ignorance of all negative comments, expressions, and discouragements.

4. A friendly alliance with two or more persons who encourage you to follow through with your plans.

Winners stay the course – they persevere in the face of obstacles; they challenge themselves to get better, to grow. If you continue with your daily disciplines for a long-enough period of time, you will succeed because you outlasted failure, you outlasted defeat, you were patient enough to accomplish everything you set out to do, you completed a journey that defies measurement, and you are now part of the 3% which everyone will remember you for. Winners follow the Tenets of Perseverance and instill them into their team. As a winner, you have perfected the virtue of patience found in the alphabet of...
The Language of Winners!

Chapter 17

QUEST –

When you discover your mission, you will feel its demand. It will fill you with enthusiasm and a burning desire to get to work on it.

~ W. Clement Stone

Quest [kwest] *Origin*: c.1300, "a search for something" (esp. of judicial inquiries or hounds seeking game), from O.Fr. queste (Fr. quête), prop. "the act of seeking," from M.L. questa "search, inquiry," alteration of L. quæsitus, pp. of quærere "seek, gain, ask" (see query).[126]

- • -

IN CHAPTER 5, I SUGGESTED THAT YOU SHOOT FOR THE MOON – and if you don't get there, you will land amongst the stars; that is still a great place to be. However, not everybody is fearless like you; not everyone wishes to leave the protection that the ozone layer provides for us on Earth. But suppose you have begun to make some positive changes in your life, you have started on a mission of personal improvement, and you have put in motion a well thought-out plan. Now, you are ready to begin your journey – your journey to the moon.

John R. Noe, in his book *Peak Performance Principles for High Achievers*, says that in order to embark on a great quest you must make no small plans. "Great plans and high goals attract big people,"[127] he says. Now, imagine NASA had made small plans when preparing for its first mission to the moon. This is what the prospective astronaut recruits may have heard: "Gentlemen, we are going to attempt to get a man off the ground and see how far we can shoot him into the air. We might eventually even try to break out of the earth's atmosphere, and see how far we can go into space."[128] Would *you* want to be amongst that group of astronauts? Do you believe anybody in their right mind would volunteer for a mission with so much insecurity and negative language?

On the other hand, because President Kennedy put pressure by giving a direct command of making no small plans, NASA officials confidently declared, "We are going to send a man to the moon during the next decade. Who wants to be the first person in history to walk on the lunar surface?"[129] Now, that's a quest that attracted the most brilliant astronauts simply because NASA utilized *the language of winners* to set the stage.

However, would you like to know the secret to *always* reaching the moon and never falling short? Winners know the secret. Here it is: constant course corrections, continually adjusting the set of your sail, relentlessly fine-tuning your route, incessantly re-evaluating your direction, and always learning from your mistakes. And then, never ever quitting, staying the course, and being persistent in your quest. That is the secret.

Jeff Olson, in his audio book *The Slight Edge*, shares a literal example of how the Apollo rocket reaches the moon.[130] He says the spacecraft travels nearly a quarter of a million miles to make contact with the moon... and pretty much 97% of the time it is off course! That's right, with the most sophisticated technology and engineering available, with the most finely calibrated instruments anywhere, and with the smartest scientists around, the rocket is right only 2-3% of the time. In other words, for every ½ hour of flight time, it is on course a mere sixty seconds! So, if this high-tech vessel has to constantly correct its direction twenty-nine minutes out of every thirty minutes – and it succeeds in landing on the moon – then, does it not make sense that you can probably do better than that?

You can experience moments of uncertainty, periods of lack of focus, you can go on sabbatical, you can stumble and fall – and you can still get back on course and straighten out your life, you can refocus, you can return from your sabbatical, and you can definitely get up, dust yourself off, and keep working toward your dreams. You are a winner, and you can do it! Others see it in your eyes. You are committed – you are on a mission and you will not be denied.

It is said that every morning in Africa a lion awakens and goes on a hunt for food. It knows that it must outrun the slowest gazelle, or else it risks starvation. By the same token, every morning in Africa a gazelle awakens and goes in pursuit of not becoming a meal. It knows that it must outrun the fastest lion, or else it risks being eaten. Whether you are physically strong like a lion or physically weak like a gazelle, when the sun rises you know in your heart and in your soul that you are on a quest for survival – either to prevent starvation or to prevent becoming a meal. And yes, you *are* running – but you are running to achieve your mission for the day, every day.

And sometimes, you are not even aware that you are in pursuit of something remotely related to self-realization, self-improvement, self-discovery, or self-control. That is exactly what happened to me back in September of 1976.

Thursday night during Orientation Week at Brown University was known as Activities Night. That evening, all the extracurricular clubs from campus went all out and put on their demonstrations in order to recruit new members. My brother and two of his sophomore friends joined me so I would not go alone. One of my new friends, Carlos Mamani, from Perú, desperately pleaded with us for someone to sign up with him for the Brown Karate Club. Nobody was biting – and because it seemed to me that he truly wanted this and he was about to shed a tear, I said I would go with him. I knew nothing of *organized* fighting, but I knew what I saw, and I saw Carlos dying if he didn't do this. We signed up at the appropriate booth, took our flyers with the class schedules, and agreed to show up for the first class the following week.

One hour before Karate class on Monday, September 21st, I called Carlos and said, "Carlos, you ready?" His reply was unexpected; he said, "Nah... I have a lot of homework. You go – I'll catch up with you later." What? I said, "Carlos, *you* were the one that wanted to sign up! Hey, I saw your eyes – you can't fake that!" I insisted but he stuck to his guns.

When I hung up the phone I decided I would not go. After all, I was really doing it for him and he couldn't make it... this time. And then a little light bulb appeared above my head – *ding!* I've got it! I will show up, I won't like it, and then I don't have to show up again. It was the perfect plan – plus, I did not want to start my college career on the wrong foot. After all, I had signed up on the dotted line, so the least I could do is show up, right? I was a responsible young man, so I did the right thing – I showed up... and I absolutely loved it! Carlos, by the way, *never* showed up.

And now, 36 years later, when people ask me why I started the martial arts, instead of the typical answer like *to get in shape*, or *for self-defense*, or even *to learn to kick some butt*, my response is always, "I joined karate to help a friend. It turns out, my friend helped me!"

Certainly, the martial arts have opened many doors of opportunity for me; they have allowed me to develop some deep, life-long relationships; they have helped me focus on my goals and they have enhanced my rate of success; they helped me survive medical school and Residency training; they have given me the confidence and discipline necessary to influence others in a positive way; they have literally taken me around the world; they have permitted me to take you in this reading expedition; they have taken me to the top of the mountain many times – and, let me tell you, it truly is an exciting journey!

As I have found out, giving of yourself and expecting nothing in return can be a very rewarding and worthwhile mission. It can change the entire direction of your life. Likewise, while on this quest, it is imperative that winners learn valuable communication skills. In fact, Les Brown says, "Your ability to communicate is an effective tool in your pursuit of your goals, whether it is with your family, your co-workers, or your clients and customers." Indeed, you must be able to convey clear and concise messages to your intended audience if you wish to reach significant degrees of achievement.

Winners are on a mission – they are totally driven, focused, and eager to get back on task – and others know it because they see it in their eyes. Winning is about the journey and its constant course corrections, not about the destination. Winners are in search of self-improvement and self-realization, and they are persistent in this quest. Winners know that if they get off-track, they can reset their sail and adjust their course by communicating effectively through... **The Language of Winners!**

Chapter 18

RESPONSIBILITY –

With great power comes great responsibility.
~ Ben Parker

Responsibility [ri-spon-suh-bil-i-tee] *Origin*: "condition of being responsible," 1787, from <u>responsible</u> + <u>-ity</u>.[131]

Responsible [ri-spon-suh-buhl] *Origin*: 1590s, "answerable (to another, for something)," from Fr. responsible, from L. responsus, pp. of respondere "to respond" (see <u>respond</u>). Meaning "morally accountable for one's actions" is attested from 1836. Retains the sense of "obligation" in the Latin root word.[132]

Respond [ri-spond] *Origin*: c.1300, respound, from O.Fr. respondere "respond, correspond," from L. respondere "respond, answer to, promise in return," from re- "back" + spondere "to pledge"[133]

– • –

IN HIS BOOK, *Outliers*, Malcolm Gladwell cites a case study where the linguists Ute Fischer and Judith Orasanu gave the following scenario to a group of airplane captains and first officers:[134]

> *You notice on the weather radar an area of heavy precipitation 25 miles ahead. [The pilot] is maintaining his present course at Mach .73, even though embedded thunderstorms have been reported in your area and you encounter moderate turbulence. You want to ensure that your aircraft will not penetrate this area. Question: What do you say to the pilot?*

The test group was given six different choices in order to persuade the pilot to change course and avoid the rough weather. In decreasing order, from strongest to weakest influence, they are:[135]

1. *Command:* "Turn thirty degrees right." This command is direct and to the point – analogous to a physician yelling out, "An amp of bicarb, STAT!" during a Code Blue in the Emergency Ward. There is no room for misunderstanding here.

2. *Crew Obligation Statement:* "I think we need to deviate right about now." The "I think" portion makes the speaker sound unsure of himself; by using "we," the speaker begins to defuse the responsibility; "right about now" is vague – it doesn't address the urgency of the condition.

3. *Crew Suggestion:* "Let's go around the weather." This suggestion is akin to an invitation for the pilot to join the speaker on a leisurely walk around the block when they get home...assuming they make it out of this alive.

4. *Query:* "Which direction would you like to deviate?" This inquiry reminds me of the casualness and we've-got-all-the-time-in-the-world mentality of "Where would you like to go eat tonight?" And because it is giving 100% of the options to the pilot, it admits that the speaker is definitely not in charge.

5. *Preference:* "I think it would be wise to turn left or right." Once again, the "I think" preface puts doubt on the speaker; "it would be wise" could be translated as "it would be sensible, but not necessary...only if you want to"; "turn left or right" is the noncommittal mark of someone who's not a winner; plus, there's no urgency when you give several options.

6. *Hint:* "That return at twenty-five miles looks mean." This is the worst of the choices. It is as if you were playing a game and you utter, "I'll give you a hint... and then you try to guess what I'm thinking and what I'm really trying to say, okay?"

The results revealed that individuals in positions of power will choose stronger statements because they speak like winners – with authority, confidence, and to the point. Thus, the captains overwhelmingly said they would give the command as listed in option number 1: "Turn thirty degrees right." On the other hand, the first officers invariably chose the weakest response; they were talking to their superiors and they opted to downplay the situation. The first officers put everyone in jeopardy because their hint – "That return at twenty-five miles looks mean" – almost sounds like a what-shall-we-talk-about-next? type of conversation, not like there's a life or death dilemma upon them.

It is evident that flying an aircraft is an enormous responsibility – you have been entrusted with multi-million dollar machinery and equipment, and with the lives of your passengers, to say the least. Nonetheless, subordinate co-pilots must be dependable and brave enough to be capable of issuing the strongest statement possible in the face of danger – lives depend on it.

Some say that "responsibility" is the ability to respond in the best way possible to what life throws at you at that particular moment. Whether it is a child wanting a little bit of your attention, or a crisis necessitating a lot of your attention, it behooves you to be reliable enough to fully engage in both scenarios to the best of your ability. In the final analysis, "the only people who count are those who can be counted on." ~ Henry F. Cope

Who can you count on to be there when you need them? Are they responsible? or are they only entitled to their rights? You see, in America we value our Constitutional rights. And if we talk about rights we also have to talk about the responsibilities that go with those rights. In *The Last Lecture*, fellow Brown alumnus, Randy Pausch says, "Rights have to come from somewhere, and they come from the community. In return, all of us have a responsibility to the community."[136] This echoes President Kennedy's famous words during his inaugural address in 1961 when he uttered, "Ask not what your country can do for you – ask what you can do for your country."

And at the start of each semester at Carnegie Mellon University, Randy Pausch had his Computer Science students sign an agreement delineating their rights and responsibilities. In the agreement, "they had to agree to work constructively in groups, to attend certain meetings, to help their peers by giving honest feedback. In return, they had the right to be in the class and to have their work critiqued and displayed."[137]

A great parallel to this approach is the Personal Development Agreement I ask my private martial arts students to sign once a year. As I mention in my book, *Tae Kwon Do for Everyone*, "The ultimate goal... is personal growth and development."[138] My belief is that they can learn kicking and punching from any of a number of people – that's not the point; the point is that I am committing to guiding my students in the right direction, helping them become better human beings. Indeed, our agreement is not the typical "karate contract," and because of that, many students have a difficult time signing on when they realize they have to be accountable.

Another fine example of "responsibility" is included in *The Last Lecture*. Randy tells the story of his Little League baseball commissioner father, who was having trouble gathering volunteer umpires. The elder Pausch then did something brilliant: "Instead of getting adults to volunteer, he had the players from the older-age divisions serve as umpires for the younger kids. He made it an honor to be selected as an ump."[139] And the benefits of this stroke of genius were: the older kids realized how challenging the role of an umpire can be, they developed a new appreciation of umpiring, and they complained less and less to the umpires of their own games; the younger kids, on the other hand, witnessed older role models who had embraced volunteering and who were demonstrating responsibility towards their league, their sport, their community, and towards each other. These kids were growing up; they were showing how responsible they can be; they were living examples of the sage words of Jim Rohn when he taught, "The day you graduate from childhood to adulthood is the day you take full responsibility for your life."[140]

Winners take responsibility seriously; they understand the level of confidence, directness, and urgency that must be utilized for emergent situations. Winners know the difference between responsibility and rights; they are willing to be accountable because they value the greater picture. Winners embrace personal improvement on a consistent basis because when they take full responsibility for their actions, their chances of growth and development are enhanced. Winners concur with Brian Tracy when he says, "The happiest people in the world are those who feel absolutely terrific about themselves, and this is the natural outgrowth of accepting total responsibility for every part of their life." Dependability, trustworthiness, and being there when you need them are signs of winners who have adopted...**The Language of Winners!**

Chapter 19

SALES – Part I

Here is a simple but powerful rule: always give people more than they expect to get.

~ Nelson Boswell

Sales [seylz] *Origin*: late O.E. sala "a sale," from O.N. sala "sale," from P.Gmc. *salo (cf. O.H.G. sala, Swed. salu, Dan. salg), from root *sal-, source of *saljan (cf. O.E. sellan; see sell). Sense of "a selling of shop goods at lower prices than usual" first appeared 1866. Salesman is from 1523.[141]

Sell [sel] *Origin*: O.E. sellan "to give," from P.Gmc. *saljanan (cf. O.N. selja "to hand over, deliver, sell;" O.Fris. sella, O.H.G. sellen "to give, hand over, sell;" Goth. saljan "to offer a sacrifice"), perhaps a causative form of the root of O.E. sala "sale." One of the first things a student of Old English has to learn is that the word that looks like sell usually means "give." Meaning "to give up for money" had emerged by c.1000. An O.E. word for "to sell" was bebycgan, from bycgan "to buy." Slang meaning "to swindle" is from 1597. The noun phrase hard sell is recorded from 1952.[142]

— • —

WE ARE ALL IN SALES! As humans, we are constantly selling one thing or another. A child who manipulates his parents into buying him a toy has closed the sale. A young man who is courting a young lady and woos her into being his girlfriend just inked the deal. More than any product or any service, we sell ourselves. People who like us, who trust us, and who believe we can bring them value, will buy into us – regardless of the product or service we're pitching.

Think of sales as a school essay. In order for the essay to even have a chance at a good grade, it must consist of three basic components: the introduction, the body, and the conclusion. Likewise, your sales presentation should consist of those same three component parts. They may have different terminology – for instance, the essay's *body* may be known as *the sales pitch*, and the essay's *conclusion* may be known as *the sales close* – but their functions are pretty much the same.

Let's take a closer look at the different parts of the sales process.

The Sales Introduction:

Sales guru Tom Hopkins gives us some advice in the October 2010 *SUCCESS* CD. If talking to a couple about financial services, he says the introduction could go something like this:[143]

> *John and Mary, we've been fortunate to help millions of families create more wealth, eliminate debt, and build financial freedom. But I always like to begin by saying, 'It's okay if this is not for you and don't be afraid to tell me No – because, if you say No I'll accept that, but hopefully you'll know some other folks that might benefit from what I'm here to share with you tonight.' So let's just relax, have fun, and let me tell you how I can get you out of debt sooner, and build financial freedom so your golden years are lived in dignity, and we all want that, don't we?*

With this introduction, Tom Hopkins increases the likelihood of making the sale because he accomplishes two things before he *ever* begins the sales presentation: 1) he alleviates a lot of the sales-related pressures his prospects may have had, and 2) he plants the seed of hope for a brighter tomorrow. He starts off by addressing the prospects by their names, which is always a great idea. He also brings credibility by revealing to the couple, in the first sentence, a little bit of his company's success.

Next, he eases their mind by saying it may not be for them and if it is not, he would appreciate referrals. The introduction winds down when he reinforces that they will have a good time and alludes to them working smarter, not harder. Finally, he brings peace of mind when he directs the couple's attention to the future and he gets them to agree with him when he says, "by the way, we all want that, don't we?" If the couple does not agree on this point, they will feel totally inadequate and uncomfortable because living in dignity and with peace of mind is something so pure and noble, as Tom suggests. So, yes, they will probably want to agree with him and will also probably come to the conclusion that they like him because of how he's made them feel, so far.

In another scenario, Mary is your potential client and before you start your business presentation, she notifies you that she's not going to buy anything. Here's what Tom Hopkins recommends as a possible introduction in this case:[144]

> *Mary, first of all, thank you for that input. And we are an educational company, meaning: I educate people as to the benefits of our business machine, and what I'd like to do is give you all the information I can, and then if you feel you have to say No that's fine. But, hopefully, you can say Yes – and if you can, then I promise you this: I'll give you the finest quality product, the best service of any person who's ever been*

a representative for you, so if you don't mind, could you just say to yourself, "Hey, Tom is here. He's investing his time away from his family. He's here to give us information." So, let's just have some fun. And I'll do my best to share with you the latest technology in the field of business machines. Would that be okay?

Instead of putting a wedge between them because of Mary's announcement prior to the presentation, Tom Hopkins brings himself closer to his prospect by remembering and saying her name, and thanking her for that information. Not getting upset impresses Mary, and she wants to hear more. Next, Tom diffuses Mary's stress, due to her preconceived notion that he's a salesman, by telling her he's there to *educate* – insinuating that he's not there to sell. He's also subtle, yet effective, when he mentions he'd like to give her "all the information" he can because he's really saying to her, "Mary, after I give you 100% of the information, you'll be able to make an intelligent decision because you're well-informed about this. You are educated!"

After that, Tom promises the best product and service to Mary if she, hypothetically, says *Yes*. So, he's already put a *Yes* in her mind even before starting the sales pitch! In the next sentence, he reiterates that he's not there to sell, he's there to educate...but he pretends Mary is the one saying this. And, by the way, he's also here when he could be with his family – so, why not pay attention and be nice to him? *Besides, he's being really nice to me!* is what Mary is now thinking.

"Let's have some fun," is more ammunition to put Mary at ease, so Mary can bring her guard down. "I'll do my best," assures Mary that his effort, energy, and enthusiasm during the presentation will not be deterred just because she voiced a *No* at the beginning. He finishes by making Mary feel more important because he's asking her for permission before he starts. You see, Mary believes she's in control – and she also believes she's not going to buy, but maybe, just maybe...she will now.

The Sales Pitch:

Many prospects will disrupt your sales pitch despite your best efforts to give the entire presentation without interruptions. Sometimes they will have legitimate questions, other times they will stop you simply to throw your rhythm off, to test you and see if you truly know your stuff, and still other times it is because they have an objection.

As we saw in the above example, objections can come at you out of nowhere and at any time during the sales process. Consequently, you have to be ready. Tom Hopkins gives us suggestions on how to overcome two common objections:[145]

Objection #1: I can get it cheaper!

Tom Hopkins: Oh, that may well be true, John. And by the way, in today's economy we all want the most for our money. But a truth I've learned over the years is the lowest price is not always what we really want. You see, I believe people look for three things when making any type of investment: 1) the finest quality, 2) the best service, and 3) the lowest price. And in all my years of researching products, I've never seen a product that can offer all three. The finest quality and the best service, for the lowest price. And I'm curious, John, for your long-term happiness, which of the three would you be most willing to give up? The fine quality? Excellent, excellent service? Or maybe a few pennies a day with a lower price?

When somebody objects, the first thing you should do is avoid a confrontation, avoid arguing. The moment you agree with the opposition, you have disarmed him. You are not here to fight, you are here to educate. Thus, when your answer is modeled after Tom Hopkins' response, you will sound smart, confident, and accessible to your customers. They will know that if they call, you will be there to service them with a smile.

Objection #2: It's a bad economy.

Tom Hopkins: When there's a dip in the economy, one thing I've learned is that some of the greatest companies in our country today built their strength and took market share during economically tough times. And in a way, the reason for that is, there's less competition, many people are not doing their best right now in the field, and so I think you might have an advantage Mr. Johnson, by looking at our company and saying, "because it's a tough economic time, now might be the time to get ahead of the competition and take advantage of some of the specials that we offer today." Because cycles are part of our economic society and if we can get ahead of the cycle, and I think our product can help you do that, when this thing gets going and turned around, you're going to leave the competition in the dust. And based on truth, that's something we should do – don't you agree?

Once again, you avoided a confrontation and you concurred that the economy *is* bad. And because your response is intelligent and you say it with conviction, your prospect is simply astonished. You finish your educational response by asking a question that puts your prospect on the spot, because his answer will undoubtedly bring him to your side.

Still, you have to be ready to back-up your statements. For example, what if your prospect questions the validity of your explanation and wants you to name some of those *great companies who took market share* during a bad economy and explain how they did it? If you have been listening to the *SUCCESS* CDs or if you have been reading this book, you are definitely equipped with a great answer. And you start off by saying, "That's a great question, Mr. Johnson!" or "Mr.

Johnson, I'm glad you asked!" or "Thank you, Mr. Johnson, for showing me that you are truly interested in improving your family's economic condition."

You can then rephrase what world-renowned economist, Paul Zane Pilzer, told Darren Hardy in his *SUCCESS* CD interview of September 2009.[146] Paul reminds us of what Amazon did in October of 2008, during the worst economic crisis of our times. When other companies complained about Christmas sales being down due to the recession, Amazon started working harder than ever before. They called their vendors and renegotiated new deals, they worked longer hours, and above all, they did not complain. The result: Amazon's fourth quarter sales in 2008 went up by 17%! – and they didn't just reduce costs, their profits increased by 11%! Amazon took advantage of everyone else admitting defeat, they capitalized on other companies' inactivity, they did not allow bad economic times to discourage them, they got focused and sprang into action, achieving tremendous earnings in a collapsing economy! They heeded Henry Ford's advice when he said, "It has been my observation that most people get ahead during the time that others waste."

Winners are awesome salespeople – they can make their prospects feel at ease with a friendly smile and a calming introduction, they can deliver an impeccable sales pitch, they can handle objections with confidence, clarity, and conviction, and above all, they can close the deal...over and over again! Winners are constantly selling and they understand that, first and foremost, they are selling themselves before they can sell any product or service. Winners are masters of sales once they've mastered... **_The Language of Winners!_**

SALES – Part II *(The Sales Close)*

If there were no problems, most of us would be unemployed.
~ Zig Ziglar

I REMEMBER ONE OF MY EARLIEST SALES EXPERIENCES at the age of 7. My family had just immigrated from México to the US and we were back visiting some relatives in México, after only a few weeks. Well, my 8 year old brother and I got a hold of some of my dad's cash receipts and we happened to have them with us, in our pockets.

When we met with our buddies whom we hadn't seen for a couple of weeks, they were eager to find out all about America. Logically, we had not been in the school system in the US long enough to learn anything substantial, yet my brother and I were already fluent in that new, scary language from up north – English. Right! Our friends would ask something, and we'd give them the English translation. It was incredible! My brother and I were on a roll! We were coming up with all sorts of supposedly-English words. Our friends were in awe. They would ask, "¿Cómo se dice gato en inglés?" (Translation: "How do you say cat in English.") Then, my sales associate and I would look at each other and silently agree on whatever first came out of our mouths. "Gah-toe," one of us would say. "Yeah, that's what I was going to say!" the other would agree. After about half hour, we had successfully done as Shakespeare did throughout his career – we'd invented some fascinating words for the world to decipher.

My brother and I had sold our friends on the fact that we'd just mastered a new language in a few short weeks. "It's really easy," we added. We had them. Their eyes were big, their mouths were shaped into circles, and their ears appeared crimson, probably from all the blood rushing to their auricles. Too many words hitting their ears, causing irritation. That was the only reasonable explanation we could come up with. Despite all these physical irregularities, they were a very receptive audience. Yes, we had 'em in our little kids' palms. They liked us, and they believed us! Our credibility was rock solid. So naturally, it was now time to *Release the Secret Weapon!* Although nobody yelled, that's the battle cry my brother and I heard in our little sales minds.

"Have you ever seen American money?" we asked. "No, no –" they quickly answered, in anticipation of more great news. "You want to see it?" "Yes, yes – hurry! Show us!" they yelled.

We needed to demonstrate total control of the transaction, so we said, "Calm down, calm down. Don't get all excited. It's just money." "Yeah," someone said, "but it's *gringo* money!"

Again, my sales partner and I spoke to each other with our eyes for a split second, then we *showed 'em the money!* Of course, a booklet of sales receipts had no real cash value then – well, I guess it doesn't have any cash value now, either. "How much is it?" asked one. "The funny thing about *gringo* money," I said, "is that you can write anything you want in this line, and then that's the money the bank gives you!" A long pause ensued, and then, "Nah!"

"Sure!" we said in unison. "Want to bet?" "No," they all said or shook. "Well, I guess we'll just have to keep this book, then," we said, as we were about to put it away. "Okay, okay! We believe you!" they said, stopping the book from disappearing forever. "Yeah, yeah!" they echoed each other.

I tore one receipt from the book and said, "¡Diez centavos!" (Translation: "Ten cents!"). Cash receipts and coins exchanged hands until we ran out of receipts. I believe it was a pack of ten, minus one or two that dad had used. [*Note: Ten Mexican cents at a time when 12.5 pesos equals one U.S. dollar, or 12 ½ Mexican cents equals one US cent, is not a lot of money. We were actually getting less than one US cent per receipt, but it was fun!*]

My sales partner and I had successfully closed on about 8 or 9 sales! Nearly an entire Cash Receipt booklet of sales in one outing! We were a powerful one-two combination! We were a sales force to be reckoned with! And my brother feared our parents were going to reckon with us real soon. We both knew we weren't supposed to take the book, but we did it anyway. So, after we told our gentler, kinder mom what we'd done, we got our answer. We could keep the money! She would, however, have to speak with dad, to explain to him and to calm him down. I guess her pride in what we had accomplished far outweighed any anger she could have felt toward us for taking the receipt book without permission. Mom was proud of her two little salesmen, her two little sharks!

This reminds me of one of my favorite TV shows, *Shark Tank*, a reality-type of program in which entrepreneurs pitch their idea of a business model to five wealthy investors (i.e., the Sharks) in the hopes of striking up a deal. The entrepreneur asks for an investment amount in exchange for a percentage of ownership in the business. The Sharks may or may not want to invest – many times, heated negotiations take place between Shark and Entrepreneur, but also cut-throat competition between Shark and Shark! And like real sharks, these Shark investors have a keen sense of olfaction, for they are able to detect even a single drop of money as soon as it lands in the *Shark Tank!* I simply love this show because I get to learn from these negotiations.

Here's the disclaimer at the beginning of the show: *The following are actual negotiations between entrepreneurs and investor "Sharks." The Sharks invest their own money at their discretion.*

The above story about my childhood had been archived for many years – it is amazing what can trigger a dormant memory to wake up. I remembered it on January 27, 2012, when I watched an episode of *Shark Tank* and heard an entrepreneur talk about his childhood. When I heard him say "ten cents," the floodgates opened and I relived that particular part of my childhood. However, what followed on the show was so good, I thought I would include it here, as it gives us a great example of the sales close.[147]

> **Entrepreneur:** I'm an expert sales professional. I can sell anything to anyone, and I've always hit my quota. (I've) been in the top 2% of every firm I've ever worked for, and I've won every sales performance award there is to win. When I was 5 years old, I would sell pencils out of my parents' house, for 10 cents apiece to my neighbors – I've been selling ever since. That's why I created – *(then he names his product).*
>
> ...I've developed the system to get you in front of the *real* decision maker who can make the buy – who can say *Yes.*

> ...Give me a C performer with a solid work ethic and I promise you, my system will teach them to close more deals than the smartest person in any room.
>
> ...I'm here for one reason – to close *this* deal. What questions can I answer for you?

After a few comments back and forth, Robert Herjavec put in his two cents' worth.

Robert Herjavec: Isn't that really what you're selling today? You're selling yourself.

Entrepreneur: Not at all – I'm selling my system and my intellectual capital.

A while later, and still not convinced, Daymond John requests more proof from the sales expert.

Daymond John: Being a sales person is about being adaptive. Do me a favor; can you sell me this pen? (*gives him his pen*) Sell us this pen right here.

Entrepreneur: Absolutely. (*takes the pen*) So, Daymond – thank you for your time. I've got a great product for you today and it's this beautiful pen right here. So, the features of it are: it's shiny, it's gonna fit nice in your hand, and people are gonna be impressed. But the *impact* that you're missing, is that this pen is gonna help change your life, because when you sign your deal with me, you're gonna be a very

	wealthy man – wealthier than you are right now. This pen, and this is where everybody gets confused –
Daymond John:	Sell it to me!
Entrepreneur:	People focus on the features –
Daymond John:	Tell me when you're done with the sale. I just want to see if I'm impressed. That was it?
Entrepreneur:	That's it.
Mark Cuban:	Well, you haven't gone for the close yet.
Entrepreneur:	The impact is *you*, inking the deal with me.
Daymond John:	(I) hated it! I'm out.

A few more comments back and forth, and then Mark Cuban decides to make an offer.

Mark Cuban:	I'm gonna ask you a very simple question – I'm gonna go for the close – if I offer you 90,000 for 40% of your company, right now will you say yes? [*Note: The entrepreneur came into the* Shark Tank *asking for precisely that – $90,000 for 40% equity.*]
Entrepreneur:	(*turns to the other Sharks*) Is that the only offer on the table?
Mark Cuban:	That's not what I asked.

Daymond John:	(*to no one in particular*) That's what he's asking for – why wouldn't he do the deal?
Mark Cuban:	Do you want to sell something or do you not?

The entrepreneur continues to talk to the other investors and one by one, the Sharks swim away from his deal. And now, there is only one investor left, Mark Cuban. By the way, he's also the only one who made an offer. The entrepreneur finally turns his attention to the Shark with the offer and this is what ensues.

Entrepreneur:	Mr. Cuban, what do we need to do right now to ink a deal? Because you know and I know this can work.
Mark Cuban:	(*long pause*) I want it to sink in on you... (*pause*) very, very hard, so it just reverberates through your body. What was my last question to you?
Entrepreneur:	Would I take the 90,000 for 40%.
Mark Cuban:	You had a chance to close, didn't you? And instead, you diverted your whole attention. You out-taught all of America one of the biggest mistakes sales people make. When they have the deal in front of them, you should just shut up and take the deal!
Robert Herjavec:	Halleluiah.

Mark Cuban: Instead of keep on selling. And you kept trying to sell.

Entrepreneur: So, do you like the idea? Do you think it can work? And would you want to see a net increase in 30-50% in your company?

Mark Cuban: Again, what was my question to you? Of course, I like the deal. Of course, I like the opportunity, which is why I offered you a chance to close it. The problem is, you basically took the whole thing for granted.

Entrepreneur: I didn't take it for granted – not one bit.

Mark Cuban: You blew it. You had the deal. It was in your hand. I was ready to close. I would have written you the check.

Entrepreneur: Mark, it still is! (*raises index finger*) It still is, Mark!

Mark Cuban: I'm not giving you an objection and asking for a reply. I'm just telling you that I'm out.

Wow! The expert salesman could not make the sale. Let's analyze what transpired and learn from this case study.

First, the salesman gave his accolades during his introductory remarks. That's good, because he wanted to make sure the investors knew of his strong sales background. Many times, others won't know what you have accomplished if you don't tell them. And then, at the end of his introduction, he said he was there for one reason, *to close this deal*. Ergo, he knew *why* he was there. Great salespeople know at the outset exactly what their goal is; they have a game plan, a strategy to make the sale. He asked for a certain amount, and he knew what wiggle room he was giving himself.

Next, Robert Herjavec stated something that all salespeople are taught: *you are selling you!* The fact that the salesman disagreed with Robert is very telling because it reveals a lethal void in his cognitive and sales process. In fact, most customers make two major buying decisions, and in the same order, before *ever* genuinely considering whether to buy your products and/or services.[148] The first decision is always whether or not to "buy" the salesperson – you. Second, whether or not to "buy" into the company that you represent. Therefore, during the time that you are "selling you," you should strive to create and build rapport, while simultaneously learning how what you have, what you represent, what you are selling, can solve his problems.

Daymond John then uses a common interview technique – he tells the salesman, who at the age of 5 sold pencils to his neighbors, to sell him a similar tool, a pen. Many times, this request catches the interviewee by surprise. The interviewer uses this strategy to gauge: sales proficiency, command of language, posturing and non-verbal communication, creativity, and your ability to think on your feet. The fact that the salesperson focused on the pen's features instead of finding out what Daymond's needs were, points to another fatal flaw in his sales approach.

The following is a theoretical dialogue that would have rendered better sales results:[149]

Entrepreneur:	Thank you for seeing me in such short notice, Daymond. As you know, I'd love to tell you all about this beautiful pen, but in order for me to do the *best* job I can, I would need to know a little more about your business needs. Is it okay if I ask you a few questions first?
Daymond John:	(*slightly amused*) Sure – go ahead.
Entrepreneur:	Thank you, Daymond. First, can you tell me how you usually correspond with others?
Daymond John:	Well, for business matters I use my PC or e-mails, for personal matters I usually text, and for branding I tweet.
Entrepreneur:	Good – so, aside from your computer or cell, what other forms of written communication do you do?
Daymond John:	I write a few hand-written notes, I sign lots of documents, and I especially like to endorse lots of checks – on the back.
Entrepreneur:	Great, Daymond – can you tell me a little more about the writing implements you

use in these occasions, and what you like and dislike about them?

Daymond John: Sure, I typically use that pen that you're holding. I like pens because they write easily and they are permanent, which is important for signatures and legal documents. However, I've had pens that when I put them in my pocket, they leak ink all over my shirt. And that's bad for the FUBU brand, plus it ruins my clothing.

Entrepreneur: (*laughs appropriately*) Very good, Daymond, very good. Well then, it seems to me that you could benefit from several writing implements. Your PC is necessary for your larger volumes of correspondence and for easier editing and storage of these documents. And a pen is beneficial for signatures and other permanent writings. And this *particular pen* will help protect the FUBU brand *and* keep your shirts from getting ruined from leakage. Furthermore, if you'd like, we can emboss your name, your initials, or even FUBU for promotional purposes. Of course, our embossing is always in gold, the color of riches and increased profits you'll see every time you endorse another one of those checks on the back, like you enjoy doing. How does this sound to you so far, Daymond?

> **Daymond John:** (*smiles*) Hey, I like this guy! (*suddenly gets a spike in mental acuity*) Wait – you've read Jay-el's book, *The Language of Winners!* Haven't you?

Finally, the exchange between the entrepreneur and Mark Cuban is what baffles me. Mark Cuban offered him *exactly* what he asked for – and he even said, "I'm gonna go for the close," loud enough for everyone to hear. Either the entrepreneur was totally shell-shocked by being in the presence of the Shark investors or he had another agenda. And when Mark Cuban is talking to him about closing sales and is trying to educate him, the entrepreneur is still trying to sell! He even asks if Mark Cuban would be interested in seeing profit increases of 30-50%. He never gets it. Anybody else, by now, would have probably realized he messed up, and would try to apologize. Yes, let Mark Cuban know that you know you did wrong, that you are only human, and that you hold yourself totally accountable.

The first step in learning a valuable lesson from a personal experience is admitting that you have something to learn from that experience. In the post-program comments, the salesman entrepreneur continued to talk as if all five Shark investors had made a huge mistake by not inking the deal he sought – although, at this point, I'm not sure what he sought. After the show, he stubbornly said, "When their sales ratios are down in the toilet, they're gonna wonder why – *You know what, I let one slip away.* And, they're gonna have to live with that."

A salesman who believes he "can sell anything to anyone," but refuses to accept constructive analysis from proven winners, will not get far in sales. A little bit of humility goes a long way. And yes, you can be both, the best at your craft *and* humble. In fact, in my book, *Master and Disciple*, I refer to the *Paradox of Greatness* by stating that, "True greatness can only be achieved by those who are humble."[150]

Indeed, if this salesman's potential customers watched this particular episode of *Shark Tank*, I'd speculate that they would probably skedaddle, just like the Sharks did. All this because of his inability to articulate...**The Language of Winners!**

Chapter 20

TEAM –

Individual commitment to a group effort – that is what makes a team work, a company work, a society work, a civilization work.

~ Vince Lombardi

Team [teem] *Origin*: before 900, O.E. team "set of draft animals yoked together," from P.Gmc. *taumaz (cf. O.N. taumr, O.Fris. tam, Du. toom, O.H.G. zoum, Ger. Zaum "bridle"), probably lit. "that which draws," from *taugmaz "action of drawing," from series *taukh-, *tukh-, *tug-, represented by O.E. togian "to pull, drag."[151]

- • -

LET'S START WITH THE SMALLEST TEAM POSSIBLE – a team of two – say, husband and wife. Zig Ziglar is the master, so I'll use this example from his book, *Success for Dummies*.[152] The husband has been away all week and is returning home late in the afternoon on a Friday. He is carrying a bulging briefcase and luggage in his hands, and he doesn't want to put them down to take out his keys or to ring the doorbell, so he kicks at the door as his way of announcing his arrival. But he doesn't hold back, he actually kicks it with anger and frustration, and even damages the door in the process! When his wife rushes to the door and opens it to see what all the commotion is, she is surprised to find her husband there, standing, heavily loaded with his belongings. He doesn't move, he simply announces, "I'm late because I've been to a meeting, and I'm really glad I was there. I learned some things that really bug me. I learned, for example, that there are a number of rights around this house that I have not been getting, and as a matter of fact, I've made a list of those rights. The first thing you and I are going to do is sit down and talk, because I'm telling you right now, there are going to be some changes made around here!"[153]

When he finishes his outburst, the wife responds in similar fashion: "Well, Buster, I didn't go to a meeting. I didn't need to. And I haven't written a list. I didn't' need to do that, either. It is burned indelibly into my own mind. There are some rights around here that *I* haven't been getting, so you come on in and we'll have that talk, because I agree with you that there are going to be some changes made, and you're not going to like most of them!"[154] Obviously, this couple is getting ready for battle. Not too many good things will ensue from their confrontation that's coming up.

Now, the same scenario, only this time the husband has just finished reading *Success for Dummies*, *The Language of Winners!*, and a few other self-improvement books during that week-long business trip, so he knows better. And instead of karate-kicking the door, he taps it with his foot just enough to attract the attention of his wife, who promptly opens it. Again, he stands there with all his personal effects, but this time he says, "Sweetheart, I apologize for being late, but I'm delighted to be here now. I'm late because I went to perhaps the most important meeting of our lives. In this meeting, I learned some things that really bother me. I have learned, for example, that in all probability I have not been meeting the needs that you have as my wife. Before I even unpack, I would like for us to sit down and talk. I would like for you to tell me what I can do to become the kind of husband that you deserve to have and that you thought you were getting when we married."[155]

This time when he finishes pouring his heart out to his wife, her eyes well up in tears as she says, "Actually, I've been very happy as your wife. From time to time, *I've* wondered if *I* have been meeting all the needs you have as my husband. I think it's a wonderful idea to sit down and talk."[156]

It is amazing what can happen when you put others' interests before yours; when you put the team first. Zig advocates that this principle applies to all walks of life, not just to marriage. He says it best with his memorable quote, "You can have everything in life you want if you will just help enough other people get what they want."[157]

A slightly bigger team, both in numbers and in physical size, is found in the game of basketball. And I would be remiss if I did not mention Coach John Wooden, college basketball's most successful coach, at this juncture. Many people asked him what his secret to success was, how was he able to win 7 National Collegiate Athletic Association (NCAA) titles in a row, and how did he accomplish 10 NCAA national championships during his tenure at UCLA? His response is classic – it is a typical winner's answer. He says, "There is no area of basketball in which I am a genius. None. Tactically and strategically I'm just average, and this is not offering false modesty. We won...because I was above average in analyzing players, getting them to fill roles as part of a team, paying attention to fundamentals and details, and working well with others, both those under my supervision and those whose supervision I was under. Additionally, I enjoyed very hard work. There is nothing fancy about these qualities. They have wide application and equal effectiveness in any team endeavor anywhere."[158]

Coach Wooden's comments support the familiar concept that "team" really stands for **t**ogether **e**veryone **a**chieves **m**ore!

This is so because everyone must contribute to the team's overall objectives, goals, and vision in order for the entire team to improve, to thrive, and to triumph so that their name is Legion.[159] Jim Rohn articulates it like this: "Is your contribution valuable to the whole? I'm telling you, without *you* the whole is incomplete! I'm telling you, it takes each of us to make all of us – each of us with a contribution... I'm asking you to consider yourself valuable enough to make an important contribution to all of us. And then, in return, you get to draw from all of us and the gifts that we bring to each of us. *That* is the power."[160]

Jim Rohn and Coach Wooden could have been talking to, or talking about, the Grey Belt Alliance (GBA) – my martial arts team that was formed a year after my world championship wins in Mexico in 2003. I was to take the GBA to Germany in 2005. Here's what happened: I, along with five male students, had been intensely training for nearly a year in preparation to compete at the 3-day World Organization of Martial Arts Athletes (WOMAA) World Games VI in Rosenheim, Germany. It would be my second world championship event as a competitor and their first. A few weeks prior to our trip, I asked the team to write down their specific goals for the championship and to turn them in to me at our next session.

At the beginning of our next training, each team member read his goals aloud and everyone was excited, and applauded and encouraged each other. Some of the goals were vague and *not specific* as I had requested. So, I asked them to think about it some more, zero-in on what it was they truly desired from this experience, and to re-write their goals. A day or two later I collected all their papers.

On the day of our departure, I handed out a laminated, 2-sided 8 ½ x 11 sheet to each teammate and asked that they read it out loud at least twice every day, once upon awakening and once before going to bed for the evening... during the entire trip. The sheet contained their specific, individualized goals on one side and the following memorandum on the other:

MEMO

July 11, 2005

TO: Grey Belt Alliance Team America athletes (aka, Soon-to-be World Champions)

FROM: Jay-el Hinojosa

In order to become World Champions, I recommend that everyone strive to have FUN during our trip to Germany. The fun should encompass all aspects of our trip, and not only the competition itself. Of course, have fun in moderation and don't do anything you'll regret later.

When one has fun during competition, possible restrictions to the mind or body are simply shed. They become a non-factor and thus, your best is free to be shared with the world... and that is an awesome feeling!

All of you have already put in the time, effort, and sacrifices needed to reach this level of competition. And so now, it's just a matter of remembering a few more things and you're on your way to becoming WORLD CHAMPIONS!

HAVING FUN SHALL MAKE YOU WORLD CHAMPIONS. Remember the following 'FUN' acronym.

Fundamentals
   You've trained with solid fundamentals, so show the world what great stances, great strikes, great blocks, great kicks, and great yells should look and sound like.

Union
   Our team is united and is working toward a common goal... to become World Champions! Let's support each other and together we shall reach the pinnacle of winning the highest honors that the World Games in Germany has to offer.

N'chantment
   Let's enchant the audience, the other competitors, and (above all) the judges with our:
   martial skills,
   professionalism,
   integrity,
   stage presence & charisma,
   and our attitude & humility.

The other side of my sheet, for example, was titled "Goals for Jay-el Hinojosa." It contained 8 specific goals, each one preceded by a small bullet-point box. The instructions just under the title read: "Place a check-mark when your goal has been reached." Of course, these instructions were meant for the team to *expect to succeed!*

As team leader and coach, I felt a sense of extra responsibilities and obligations, so one of my goals was, "We shall travel to Germany on July 11th and return back to our homes safely on July 19th." I was not taking anything for granted.

Another goal for me was, "My lower back and shoulders shall be pain-free during the competition." Actually, each one of us was nursing an injury or two prior to the Games – it turns out the martial arts are, in fact, a contact sport!

Team America consisted of one-hundred athletes, six of whom were our Grey Belt Alliance Team from south Texas. And our results spoke volumes about our team: 5 out of 6 of us came back as World Champions – a few of us with multiple titles!

Winners work well with others; they elevate the level of everyone around them by bringing value to the team. Winners individually commit for the greater good – thus, they maximize their efforts. Winners put the interests of others before theirs; they put the team first. Winners understand their roles as part of a team and the fact that they each make a significant contribution in order for the team to attain the results it desires. Winners share their best with the world and they have 'FUN' in the process. A winning team is one that identifies with, and sees itself as an integral part of...***The Language of Winners!***

Chapter 21

UNIVERSAL LAWS –

The best study of life is how it is – not how you wish it to be, not how you wish to rearrange it – how to take advantage of how it is.

~ Jim Rohn

Universal [yoo-nuh-vur-suhl] *Origin*: late 14c., from O.Fr. universel (12c.), from L. universalis "of or belonging to all," from universus "all together, whole, entire" (see universe). In mechanics, a universal joint (1676) is one which allows free movement in any direction; in theology universalism (1805).[161]

Universe [yoo-nuh-vurs] *Origin*: 1589, "the whole world, cosmos," from O.Fr. univers (12c.), from L. universum "the universe," noun use of neut. of adj. universus "all together," lit. "turned into one," from unus "one" + versus, pp. of vertere "to turn"[162]

Laws [laws] *Origin*: 1580-90, O.E. lagu (pl. laga, comb. form lah-), from O.N. *lagu "law," collective pl. of lag "layer, measure, stroke," lit. "something laid down or fixed," from

P.Gmc. *lagan "put, lay" (see lay (v.)). Replaced O.E. æ and gesetnes, which had the same sense development as law. Cf.¹⁶³

- • -

IN 1906, ITALIAN ECONOMIST VILFREDO PARETO MADE AN INTERESTING OBSERVATION: he noticed that 80% of Italy's land was owned by 20% of the population. He wondered if this was also true of other places, so he carried out similar surveys in a number of countries and found, much to his amazement, that the distribution patterns were comparable. He further noted that 20% of the pea pods in his garden contained 80% of the peas. These observations marked the beginning of *The Pareto Principle*, Pareto's Law, or the 80-20 rule, which seems to have universal applications regardless of the industry.¹⁶⁴

For instance, in an article by *Computer Retail News* in 2002, it was discerned that if 20% of the most-reported bugs were fixed at Microsoft, 80% of all their errors and crashes could be avoided.¹⁶⁵ Similarly, when Steve Jobs regained control of the downward spiraling Apple Inc. in 1997, one of the first things he did was to eliminate most of the product line and just focus on a few products – the ones which were bringing in most of the revenues to the company. *Oxygen: The Turnaround Magazine* says of Jobs, "He immediately sought out to clean out the Apple stable, binning a host of projects and bringing in the iMac and other design-led products...Following his return to Apple in 1997, revenue grew by 821%."[166] This strategy helped propel Apple to the stratosphere, making it the world's most valuable publicly traded company in 2011![167]

By the same token, the United Nations Development Program Report showed the following distribution of global income in 1992: the richest 20% of the world's population controls 82.7% of the world's income.[168] In regards to health care, the U.S. Department of Health & Human Services stated that in 2002, 80% of all U.S. health care expenditures were attributed to 20% of the population.[169] And in an Oregon Senate floor debate in February 2012, Senator Alan Bates said something that shocked those who were unfamiliar with the universality of the Pareto Principle: "Eighty percent of the health care dollars are spent by 20 percent of the population."[170]

In fact, certain universal principles, or laws, exist because of their widespread acceptability and applicability, and they are therefore considered to be the most valid. The adage, "What goes up must come down," follows the law of gravity to a great extent – the exception is seen when the object that goes up has enough velocity to overcome the gravitational force that's trying to keep it down. Thus, a rocket traveling to the moon – as the one we discussed in Chapter 17 – is one of the few things that generates sufficient velocity to escape the pull of gravity.

But laws also govern society – and without them, there would be chaos and anarchy. In essence, the law is an established code of conduct which guides our society in the right direction, towards prosperity. You will want to understand this next law, which will transform every area of your life if you use it wisely. It is known as the *Law of Attraction*.

The Law of Attraction is the most powerful force in the Universe. It is simple in concept but requires some dedicated practice to fully master. However, once you grasp the concept, you will be amazed at the many doors of possibility that will open up for you. The simplest definition of this law is: *like attracts like*.

This universal law is working in your life right now, whether you are aware of it or not. You are attracting people, situations, opportunities, money, employment offers, and much more into your life. *Whether you know it or not, you attracted this book into your life.* Once you are aware of this law and how it works, you can start to use it to deliberately attract what you want into your life, into your reality.

To maximize your use of the Law of Attraction, I recommend you follow the 4S plan, which is:[171]

1. *Specific*. It is important to know *exactly* what you want. For instance, instead of saying "I don't want to be poor," voice "After 12 months in business, I want to be

financially secure, generating $5,000 per month from my new business." With regards to your health, instead of saying "I don't want to be overweight," declare "I want to lose 15 pounds by February 24th."

2. *See.* You must *visualize* and feel positive about what you desire. Your mind will kick into overdrive to support those things you feel especially good about. It is easier to accomplish something you have already seen yourself accomplish.

3. *Say.* Take advantage of the power of *affirmations* to attract all that you wish towards you. Say aloud, "I am developing great relationships," "I am carving a great physique and am enjoying a healthier, more vibrant body," and "I love my new business because I'm making a positive impact in the lives of others and I get to spend more quality time with my family."

4. *Seize.* By taking *inspired action*, you can seize what you have specifically seen and said aloud. Believe it or not, the planets will align and the Universe will open ways for you to achieve what your heart desires.

In 1955, Cyril Northcote Parkinson first penned the famous line, "Work expands to fill the time available for its completion." Two years later, it became the focus of his best-selling book *Parkinson's Law: The Pursuit of Progress.*[172,173]

Practically speaking, it means that if you give yourself four months to complete work that you can do in 24 hours, then the work will "expand" (via psychological and other intangible occurrences) by subjectively becoming more complex and stressful so as to fill the entire four months! The extra time may not even be filled with more work, simply more impalpable manifestations such as increased anxiety, leading to fear and procrastination, about having to complete the work.

A few years ago, I experienced Parkinson's Law first-hand. In the Fall of 2005, I enrolled in a graduate level *Scriptwriting* class at the University of Texas-Pan American in Edinburg – I had a story I wanted to share and I knew that if I didn't put a bit of pressure on myself, it wouldn't get done anytime soon. I spoke to my professor, Dr. Jack Stanley, at the beginning of the semester to make sure we were both on the same page about the expectations for this course. I normally would not have met with my professor for something like this, but this was different – this time, I was a very busy full-time physician and I wasn't going to be able to show up during the day to an actual "class." Dr. Stanley and I agreed that my only requirement was to turn in my 90 page script at the end of the semester. Simple enough, right?

Well, *life happens* and I was swamped with work and family obligations. One afternoon, after finishing a long day at my clinic and as I started my drive home, I decided to call my professor just to find out exactly what day I should turn in my play. I figured there were about two more weeks before the end of the semester, so I wanted to give myself some cushion. When Dr. Stanley came on the line, we exchanged pleasantries and then I asked my query. With a smile (I could sense it through the cell phone) he told me, "Oh, just bring it in tomorrow by 5pm, Jay-el!" Tomorrow? I do not know how I was able to produce any coherent sounds after that tsunami hit me, but I managed to say, "Sure, Dr. Stanley, I'll... see you tomorrow before five." I hung up and the wheels in my head immediately started turning. My dilemma was straightforward: I had not started at all!

I quickly elected to *just do it*, so I made a few phone calls to change my plans. I notified my wife and advised her I would not be coming home anytime soon. I let my teenage daughters know I may be running late for school in the morning. Luckily for me, the university computer labs remained open all night. I picked up a burger on the way to the university and situated myself in front of a vacant computer. I rationalized with myself, "I can do this! The story is already in my head. I just need to put it on paper."

I took a deep breath and started typing. The keys were going at a steady pace and after a while, their sound morphed into white noise as the hours started to tick away. The noise level at the lab seemed to escalate as more and more students trickled in – it was almost like a war zone, a revolution – and I needed to survive. At one point, the computer lab got very quiet and when I looked up, I noticed the place was now empty except for me, of course. I looked at my watch and it was a few minutes after 2:00 am. My wife called to check up on me and I told her to go back sleep – she did not. She called me every hour on the hour to make sure I didn't fall asleep and mess everything up. (As if I hadn't already messed everything up.)

From about 3:00 to 6:00 am, my fingers went on autopilot and they kicked into *warp speed*. I had never experienced that type of Star Trek dimension before, or since. I wasn't even thinking what was supposed to come next – there was no time to think. I was simply sitting there in awe of what my left hand and my right hand were doing, not *because of* me but *in spite of* me. And I was not looking at the screen either – I couldn't. Those last three hours I was balling uncontrollably – not because I was scared or upset at my predicament, but because of what I sensed was happening. *This revolution was transforming into a revelation.* The story that was unfolding in front of me was deeply engaging and emotional. I was crying like a baby! Good thing the room was empty.

At exactly 6:30 am, I printed my 88 page manuscript and as I got up to pick up the printout, I felt the stiffness in my lower back and neck. I left my station, went home to shower and change, and after giving my wife a hug and a kiss, quickly left to pick up my daughters for school. I proudly showed them my finished project and Laura told me, "Dad, it's only eighty-eight pages. You need two more pages." That was the needle to my 24-hour balloon of accomplishment. Alexis, my younger daughter, advised me that I still had time because it wasn't due until 5 pm. She was right, but I told her that my full clinic schedule would not allow me to dedicate any more time to it. So, after I dropped them off at school, I hand-delivered my play to Dr. Stanley at the university.

After the dust settled and I had an opportunity to read what my fingers had transcribed, I was totally ecstatic with the results. The bravura of ten digits! Had the keyboard been a piano, my fingers would have just finished a brilliant performance of one florid passage after another for an entire evening. In essence, they had autonomously transmuted some dormant brain waves into a compelling story on paper. Ergo, three years later, *Rosi Milagros* was published as a two-act play.[174] This goes to show that you can literally become a playwright overnight!

I do not recommend this type of stress and scenario to anyone – and if I had to do it all over again, I certainly would not procrastinate like I did. What I believe happened that night, was a sort of magical *inversion* of Parkinson's Law. That's right, the law would now be structured like this: "Time expands to fill the work available for its completion!"

One additional observation regarding this intense 24-hour period: I had been writing for many years by the time I enrolled in this *Scriptwriting* class. In fact, while at Brown University, my *Personal and Reflective Writing* English instructor, Anne Huber, called me "The Master of Understatement" one day when I turned in a ten-page paper...and the assignment was a two-pager! At any rate, according to Malcolm Gladwell in his book *Outliers*, "researchers have settled on what they believe is the magic number for true expertise: ten thousand hours."[175] He quotes neuroscientist Daniel Levitin, PhD, as stating that, "...ten thousand hours of practice is required to achieve the level of mastery associated with being a world-class expert – in anything."[176] He goes on to include extensive descriptions of The Beatles, Bill Gates, and others, and of how they qualified for their ten thousand hours. But not just *any* 10,000 hours – remember "Perfect practice makes perfect" vs. "Practice makes perfect"? That's right, to qualify as experts, the 10,000 hours you put in have to entail *purposeful practice with the intent to get better at your craft*. Thus, *The 10,000-hour Rule* emerges as another one of life's universal principles that winners must be cognizant of.

Winners are predictable, like the sun – they predictably rise to the occasion just as the sun predictably rises in the east and sets in the west. Winners excel in maximizing results and minimizing set-backs by accepting and collaborating with the laws of the Universe, not by going against them. Like in the Pareto Principle, winners find a way to reach the top 20% because those are the most successful at their profession, skill, or craft. Winners are well-versed in Parkinson's Law, since they know that by assigning the proper amount of time for the completion of a task or a job, they will gain back more time and the complexity of the task will revert to its original, natural state. Winners realize there are no short cuts to success; they know about the 10,000-hour Rule and about the universality of...***The Language of Winners!***

Chapter 22

VALUE –

Service to others is the rent you pay for your room here on earth.

~ Muhammad Ali

Value [val-yoo] *Origin*: c.1300, from O.Fr. value "worth, value" (13c.), noun use of fem. pp. of valoir "be worth," from L. valere "be strong, be well, be of value" (see valiant). The meaning "social principle" is attested from 1918, supposedly borrowed from the language of painting.[177]

Valiant [val-yuhnt] *Origin*: c.1300, from Anglo-Fr. and O.Fr. valliant "stalwart, brave," from prp. of valoir "be worthy," originally "be strong," from L. valere "be strong, be well, be worth, have power, be able," from PIE base *wal- "be strong" (cf. O.E. wealdan "to rule," O.H.G. -walt, -wald "power" (in personal names), O.N. valdr "ruler," O.C.S. vlasti "to rule over," Lith. valdyti "to have power," Celt. *walos- "ruler," O.Ir. flaith "dominion," Welsh gallu "to be able").[178]

- • -

MANY PEOPLE ARE NOT GOOD SAMARITANS these days. That could be a good thing, depending on how you look at it. Say you are walking down the street and you hear someone cry *Help!* What do you do? Probably spring into action, right? Hopefully, you do...but the question is: In which direction? Do you spring into action in the direction of the yeller or in the opposite direction? Are you going to render help? Or are you doing like a banana, and splitting?

In one scenario, the *Help!* yell is a crisis – to the yeller, of course. Perhaps you envision the damsel in distress who's tied down on the railroad tracks, as in the silent movie era. You may want to quickly disassociate yourself with anyone who is in this predicament. Why? What if, while you're responding to the yeller's cry for help, you yourself get injured? Or worse yet, what if you die? On the other hand, it could have been a set up or an ambush. The yeller may seem helpless and vulnerable but, in reality, may be evil and calculating. The yeller may want your money, or your life.

Human nature tells us that whenever someone cries for help, he's already given up. He's thrown in the towel. He's now completely without help; he's *helpless*. And he needs *you* to come to the rescue, to be a hero, to be valiant, to drop everything and to willingly enter an arena that you may not be prepared to enter.

In my book, *Report Card on Rape*, I mention that yelling *Fire!* instead of *Help!* or *Rape!* can give you a better chance of someone else coming to your rescue.[179] It turns out that the threat of an actual fire to passers-by will kick in a type of self-preservation mode. What if my home or my business is on fire? Or what if I lose some*thing* or some*one* in this tragedy, even though I realize the fire seems far enough away from my property?

As a physician, I've been faced with a lot of detective work in order to arrive at an accurate diagnosis. First, I *listen* to the constellation of symptoms conveyed by a patient during an office visit. Second, I *observe* for specific signs during the physical examination and the allied health testing. And finally, I get to piece everything together to create a finalized puzzle; hopefully, one that reveals the correct diagnosis.

So, when a patient complains of things like, "I'm feeling down," "I'm tired," "Please help me," "I'm not so self-assured," "I feel so insecure," "My independence seems to vanish," I naturally think of common diagnoses like depression, anemia, diabetes, a thyroid condition, or even (with "Please help me") possible suicide ideations. One would think that pop music is the farthest thing from my mind, right? Actually, with the exception of "I'm tired," these complaints are *exact words* found in the Beatles' hit song entitled *Help!*[180] This song even led to a feature length film by the same name in 1965. Thus, it's incredible how we've gone from depression, anemia, diabetes, and thyroid disease to a hit song (and even a movie) from the Beatles! And this song/movie tandem is probably partly responsible for the word *help* having such a negative connotation within our culture. Perhaps prior to 1965, the simple question, "How can I help you?" was perfectly fine. Now, however, after nearly half a century of being bombarded with the negative words and messages associated with this song, it is feasible that our subconscious can't help but feel helpless!

"How can I help you?" will now automatically go to our negative files within our psyche. It brings to mind someone who's not supposed to be there, or someone who's doing something he's not supposed to be doing. Either way, you do not belong. Usually, an authority figure will utter these words at the most inopportune time. For example, you have just entered a place of business and you haven't even caught your breath yet when the attendant asks, "How can I help you?" Maybe you haven't made up your mind yet, or perhaps you need to view some of the items before deciding. Either way, the word "help" and the timing of the question make you feel like you want to leave.

So, instead of using the very negative word "help," one can try the empowering words "assistance" or "service." "How may I be of assistance?" or "How may I be of service?" are alternatives with a more positive insinuation. Plus, the opposite of *help* is *helpless*, which implies weakness, vulnerability, and dependence. However, there is no *service-less* as an antonym of *service* or *assistance-less* as an antonym of *assistance that* I know of.

In sports, statistics are kept for the number of assists, not the number of times you "help out." An assist is when you work as a team, allowing someone else to get the credit that you made possible; that you facilitated. You are supporting your teammate, and that is bringing value to the team. It is empowering; it is growth; it is a positive change. "Help," conversely, would not allow you to grow; it would hinder your growth because you are *dependent* on someone else doing this for you.

In our second option, we can say something like, "How may I be of service?" In essence, this servant's approach communicates to the listener, "How can I be useful to you?" or, "I am at your disposal!" or even, "Your wish is my command!" Now, you're talking, and the listener truly feels important. The message here is that you are willing to go the extra mile to make a difference, to bring value to your listener – and that's a great example of servant leadership, servant friendship, and even servant partnership. In servant leadership, the servant leader, owner, manager, and so on, is there whenever his followers or customers are in need. As a servant friend, you are there whenever your friends are in need. And as part of a servant partnership, you are there when your partner, spouse, or business associate, is in need. Zig Ziglar says it best when he says, "You are a success when you know that the greatest are those who choose to be the servants of all."

Thus, in order to achieve success, it is best not to help the helpless. Instead, try empowering others by assisting them and collaborating as a team. Try being of service, being useful, to those in need by providing more than is expected. And in reality, success can only be accomplished when you truly desire to be of service to others – and in this way, you are ultimately expressing... **The Language of Winners!**

Chapter 23

WILL –

The good or ill of a man lies within his own will.

~ Epictetus

Will [wil] *Origin*: before 900, O.E. *willan, wyllan "to wish, desire, want" (past tense wolde), from P.Gmc. *welljan (cf. O.S. willian, O.N. vilja, O.Fris. willa, Du. willen, O.H.G. wellan, Ger. wollen, Goth. wiljan "to will, wish, desire," Goth. waljan "to choose"), from PIE *wel-/*wol- "be pleasing" (cf. Skt. vrnoti "chooses, prefers,"[181]

- • -

IN HIS 1994 AUTOBIOGRAPHY, bodybuilding champion Lou Ferrigno credits four major keys for his incredible successes in life:[182]

· *self-belief*
· *consistency*

- *determination*
- *persistence*

Sound familiar? You, as a winner, will note that *The Language of Winners!* includes three of the four components in earlier chapters – the fourth inclusion within this work, *determination*, is examined in this chapter. Lou defines determination as "the will to succeed and drive forward. It is something that truly comes from within. You've got to locate it within you and cultivate your passion for the pursuit of your goal."[183]

Lou Ferrigno overcame many adversities and health issues, especially of the blood-borne variety – as in, his father. Lou was also fighting a losing battle – he was trying to please his athletically-gifted father, a man who could not be pleased. For instance, Lou was generally considered a "hitter" in baseball. However, whenever his father attended his Little League games, Lou transformed into a strike out king because he knew his father was just waiting to criticize him for something – or for anything. And when he glanced over to his father after the third strike, perhaps seeking fatherly support and backing, the elder Ferrigno would simply shake his head in disgust and go on about how he would have hit homers each and every time, had he been the batter. He even went as far as to repeatedly tell Lou, "You'll never make it as an athlete."[184]

When someone with great influence over you, such as your father, constantly degrades you, it is definitely an uphill battle to climb out of that oppressing force. Nevertheless, you must look into your heart, into your soul, to summon that power that will take you to victory. When you exert your power to choose your own actions, you are expressing your will. And because you are *electing* the direction your life will take, you have *total control* over your results, whether positive or negative. It is up to you to select wisely – do you wish to try to please others or will you follow your passion, your own drive, your "ganas" (Spanish for "desire")? You are the only one who can answer that question – and Lou Ferrigno answered it as a winner.

The Spanish word "ganas" seems to be ubiquitous in many of my motivational presentations. However, I'm not the only one that digs deep to beckon *ganas* – Edward James Olmos, in the superb 1988 film *Stand and Deliver*, portrays legendary mathematics teacher Jaime Escalante when he addresses his high school students with the following:[185]

> *There will be no free rides, no excuses. You already have two strikes against you: your name and your complexion. Because of those two strikes, there are some people in this world who will assume that you know less than you do. Math is the great equalizer... When you go for a job, the person giving you that job*

will not want to hear your problems; ergo, neither do I. You're going to work harder here than you've ever worked anywhere else. And the only thing I ask from you is 'ganas.'
(Passing one boy, he ruffles up the student's hair)
And maybe a haircut.
(Everyone laughs)
If you don't have the 'ganas,' I will give it to you because I'm an expert.

Jaime Escalante was indeed an expert at inspiring young people to achieve more than they ever imagined – and Bruce Lee was also an expert and a trailblazer in the martial arts. In his classic 1973 film, *Enter the Dragon*, one can appreciate yet another example of will, inner drive, and resolve when Han, the villain, declares to the competitors during the opening ceremonies of his global martial arts tournament:[186]

> *Gentlemen, welcome. You honor our island. I look forward to a tournament of truly epic proportions. We are unique, gentlemen, in that we create ourselves... through long years of rigorous training, sacrifice, denial, pain. We forge our bodies in the fire of our will.*

In the last sentence, Han could very well be saying, "Gentlemen, we create our reality by igniting our power within!" It is true, your will power must start from a profound place in your being. Then, it must spread like a wildfire of intensely focused activity – and if anybody tries to get too close, they will get burned with your flames because you are not about to deviate from your success journey.

Winners have the will, the drive, and determination to see the job done to completion – *tienen las ganas* (Spanish for "they have the drive")! Hungry winners are never satiated because their resolve will never allow them to give up; they wake up every morning with the passion and appetite for knowledge, for improvement, and for victory. Winners put forth the power to choose their own actions, and by doing so they *will* themselves into another dimension – the dimension of *ganas* from... **The Language of Winners!**

Chapter 24

XCUSES –

He that is good for making excuses is seldom good for anything else.

~ Benjamin Franklin

Excuses [ik-skyoos] *Origin*: early 13c., "to clear (someone) from blame," from O.Fr. escuser, from L. excusare "release from a charge," from ex- "out, away" + causa "accusation, legal action" (see cause). Meaning "to obtain exemption or release" is from mid-15c.; that of "to accept another's plea of excuse"[187] I can picture a courtroom scene where the accused is excused because he had a solid alibi (i.e., his excuse).

Cause [kawz] *Origin*: early 13c., from L. causa "a cause, reason, judicial process, lawsuit," of unknown origin. Cause célèbre "celebrated legal case" is 1763, from French.[188]

- • -

IT HAS BEEN SAID THAT SUCCESSFUL INDIVIDUALS

HAVE BIG LIBRARIES and small TVs, whereas unsuccessful people have big TVs and small libraries, or none at all. Presley Swagerty refers to TVs as "income reducers" and says that he never liked to read, that's why he taught Math for many years. He quickly adds that he now reads consistently and if he's on the road, he inserts an audio book into his "Rolling University" CD player and it's like having, for example, John Maxwell sitting next to him, mentoring him and teaching him about leadership. The *lazy* person's alternative to reading is those books on CD, he says. The main thing, however, is to put good information into your head. This will broaden your perspectives, and like Jim Rohn says, it will open up a whole new "treasure chest of possibilities" for you.

In the October 2009 *SUCCESS CD*, Jim Rohn shares his ideas on reading.[189] He says that some of the most successful people in the world have written books on exactly how they did it, and people don't read them! Yes, you can learn from your own experiences, but you can also learn from others' experiences – by reading, studying, and following the advice found in the pages of the books of winners. Like Jim Rohn, I believe you can change your life by reading a book a week, or a book a month – but read. At this precise instant, you're on the right track because you are holding and reading this book.

Jim Rohn adds, "One book might save you five years...if you read it."[190] Here's how he finishes off his powerful message on reading:[191]

> *Reading is tapping the treasure of ideas... and ideas can change any part of your life. And if you've got a good excuse not to tap the treasure of ideas, at least 30 minutes a day, or spend the money and get the book, I'd love to hear it. Some people have excuses you wouldn't believe. I say, "John, look – I've got this gold mine. I've got so much gold, I don't know what to do with it all. Come on over and dig." John says, "I ain't got a shovel." I say, "Well, John, get you one!" He says, "You know what they want for shovels?"*

It may not be a literal "gold mine," but Jim Rohn is offering his friend a job, an opportunity, perhaps some handiwork, but he has reached out and opened a door for John to walk through. And what does John do? He finds an excuse. When Jim Rohn advises his friend to get a shovel, he is really saying to him, "John, I understand you don't have the necessary tools right now, but I'm willing to wait for you; I'm willing to reserve this opportunity for you, *if* you make the effort to figure out a way to get the tools you need." Yet again, John resists the opportunity; he doesn't want to take advantage of the "gold mine" he is being offered. So, John does what he's good at – he finds another excuse. Perhaps he thought it was fool's gold.[192] Whatever his rationale, it is time to offer the gold mine opportunity to someone else – someone who will see it for what it is, an opportunity for success.

As I mentioned earlier in the book, I'm a big fan of the hit ABC show *Shark Tank*, which gives entrepreneurs an opportunity for success. On February 10th, 2012, I watched an episode where a woman entrepreneur was pitching her dog cake business to the Sharks.[193] She had been in business 4 years and only had $80,000 in sales during that period and $23,000 during the most recent year of operation. Mark Cuban, owner of the Dallas Mavericks basketball team, was one of the Sharks. He asked her why she thinks she'd only grown her business to twenty-three thousand over the past year, and this is what followed:

Entrepreneur: The thing that I lack the most is capital and connections. I've never attended a trade show because I don't have the capital for it. I can't get in front of distributors unless I go to trade shows, and that's why I'm here. I'm seeking an investment in order to be able to take my company to the next level.

Robert Herjavec: But you could have called distributors.

Entrepreneur: I *have* called distributors...

Robert Herjavec: And what do they tell you?

Entrepreneur: I don't get a return phone call.

Lori Greiner: Have you tried to go to dog pet stores? Places like that? Have you tried cold call walk-in and just say, "Would you be interested in my puppy cakes?"

Entrepreneur: A couple of times I have, uh... sales is really not my strong suit...

A while later, Mark Cuban recaps his thought process.

Mark Cuban: What you have is, I think, a good product. But you've had 4 years and you didn't feel like your back was against the wall *enough* to break through your personal barriers. You know, you told us that you weren't really a salesperson. To me, that tells me that you aren't committed enough to the product to try anything. I can't see writing a check for somebody who finds the excuse rather than finds the opportunity. So, for that reason, I'm out.

Mark Cuban's rationale was right on, and his words of wisdom reiterate what Presley Swagerty conveys as he declares, "You can make money, or you can make excuses – but you can't make both!" *Excuses* are exactly what the entrepreneur from this episode was making right from the outset. She uttered these negatives, one after the other: "I lack," "I've never," "I don't," and "I can't." These phrases obviously overpowered the other action phrase "I'm seeking" (at best, a weakly-positive counter to all the negatives) and all this negativity remained in the Sharks' minds enough for them not to want to team up with her in this venture.

Winners are committed, they are willing to do whatever it takes, and they accept full accountability for the results in their life. Winners do not make excuses; whiners do. Who would you rather be with, a winner or a whiner? Once more, my friend Presley articulates it very memorably when he says, "You've got to be a person that others want to be around. Nobody, and I mean *nobody*, wants to run around with a negative, dull, disillusioned, frustrated, cry baby."

Do not do the song and dance of negative people: do not make excuses, and YOU can be the person others want to be around. Instead, you can sing and dance with positive people: you can be optimistic, you can be enthusiastic, and you can be energetic because each and every day you will be singing, dancing, and living... **The Language of Winners!**

Chapter 25

Yo-yo –

But enough about me, let's talk about you – what do YOU think about me?

~ CC Bloom

Yo-yo [yoh-yoh] *Origin*: 1915, apparently from a language of the Philippines. Registered as a trademark in Vancoucer, Canada, in 1932, the year the first craze for them began (subsequent fads 1950s, 1970s, 1998). The toy itself is much older and was earlier known as bandalore (1824). Figurative sense of any "up-and-down movement".[194]

- • -

BECAUSE PROPS OFTEN HELP MAKE A POINT, I've utilized them frequently for my public speaking engagements. A few times, I've gone to the stage with a wooden Mexican toy called a *valero*. [The valero consists of three components: a barrel-shaped body, a hand-held stick, and a string that connects the two. The body has a small opening at the bottom, and the object of the game is to flip the barrel onto the stick. When you successfully accomplish this, you can then continue flipping it onto the stick from that position – this is called a *capirucho*.]

Naturally, the audience is intrigued with this colorful toy I hold in my hand, so I'll tell them the name of it and demonstrate how it works. Usually, I get it to go in on the first try, so everyone smiles and claps. I'll then add something like, "You know, this morning when I was getting ready to come here, I faced two choices: I could have brought my yo-yo or I could have brought my valero. I decided on the valero because this presentation, ladies and gentlemen, is not about *yo, yo, yo* – this presentation is about *you, you,* and *you!*" I point at myself when I say "yo" (which is Spanish for "me") and I point at different attendees when I say "you." Invariably, the applause starts up again and the audience is feeling pretty good about themselves – and I haven't even started my presentation!

I, the first-person pronoun, is very selfish, quite egotistical, and totally self-interested. When you are truly interested *in others*, instead of trying to be *interesting*, you will succeed. Zig Ziglar says, "You can get everything in life you want if you will just help enough other people get what they want." The secret lies in turning the spotlight on others, in genuinely giving your best effort for the benefit of your team, your family, your co-workers, your cause, or your country. You are interested in *their* success. Thus, the focus has to be bigger than one person, bigger than I.

Sometimes I remind my business associates that even The Lone Ranger had Tonto...and Silver! There just aren't enough hours in the day for one person to accomplish all the tasks that eventually add up to success at the end of the day. That's why delegating authority and empowering others is important; that's why you entrust others with smaller goals that they can achieve; that's why you leverage off other people's efforts in order to maximize your results.

As I mention in my book, *Magnets for Health*, "you push yourself so that you may EMPOWER others."[195] Of course, a residual effect from my years in medical school was the accumulation and usage of acronyms – and, yes, EMPOWER is an acronym. You EMPOWER others when you help them to:[196]

E	=	**E**mbark in the commitment ship and set their sail.
M	=	**M**odel your example so they can one day lead.
P	=	**P**artner up with you for a collaborative effort.
O	=	**O**rganize themselves and their work.
W	=	**W**ork the success plan you've shared with them.

> **E** = **E**xpect to win, expect to succeed.
>
> **R** = **R**eceive your acknowledgments, appreciations, and recognitions.

Since it's not about you – it's about empowering others – then you can focus your efforts and time on building and developing your team. As a leader, you will assist them to identify their level of commitment and once they've done that, they can then ***embark*** on their vessel and set their sail in the direction that will take them to their destination.

You lead by example and as you grow as a leader, you become worthy of being modeled. Your team will ***model*** your actions, your techniques, your command of the business plan, and your every move. And as they learn the business and its specific language, they will gain the confidence necessary to, one day, grow into leaders themselves.

When you embrace your team and become ***partners*** with them, they will realize that you are there to support them, to guide them in their journey, to collaborate with them so that they can achieve the results they desire.

Because you are a leader, you teach your team members how to ***organize*** not only themselves, but also their work and their schedule; you teach them to systematize their projects so that all the interdependent parts work as a unit.

By allowing your team to **work** the success plan you have helped them to plan out, you are empowering them; you are giving them an opportunity to win by working a proven system.

Zig Ziglar says, "You were born to win, but to be a winner, you must plan to win, prepare to win, and **expect** to win." As a leader, you will empower your team by drilling into them the expectations of winners.

Your team will get a boost of empowerment the moment they openly **receive** your appreciation for all the dedicated work they engage in; your acknowledgments, appreciations, and recognitions of your team's efforts will go a long way toward developing a winning culture.

The phrase "No man is an island" comes from the English priest, John Donne, as he convalesced from a serious illness.[197] In his 1624 work, the particular devotion that includes the following passage was subtitled, "Now, this bell tolling for another, says to me, thou must die." Apparently, John Donne thought the Grim Reaper was upon him when he wrote:[198]

> *No man is an island entire of itself;*
> *every man is a piece of the continent, a part of the main;*
> *if a clod be washed away by the sea, Europe is the less,*
> *as well as if a promontory were,*

> *as well as a manor of thy friends or of thine own were;*
> *any man's death diminishes me,*
> *because I am involved in mankind.*
> *And therefore never send to know for whom the bell tolls;*
> *it tolls for thee.*

Winners think of others first; they realize that the best way to reach the top is to bring others with you. Winners understand that *"I"* is the least important word in... **The Language of Winners!**

Chapter 26

ZEST –

Nothing great was ever achieved without enthusiasm.
~ Ralph Waldo Emerson

- **Enthusiasm** [en-thoo-zee-az-uhm] *Origin*: 1570–80; < Late Latin *enthūsiasmus* < Greek *enthousiasmós*, equivalent to *enthousí* (*a*) possession by a god, (*énthous,* variant of *éntheos* having a god within.[199] You are one with the energy of the divine.[200]

- **Passion** [pash-uhn] *Origin*: 1125–75; Middle English (< Old French) < Medieval Latin *passiōn-* (stem of *passiō*) Christ's sufferings on the cross, any of the Biblical accounts of these (> late Old English *passiōn*), special use of Late Latin *passiō* suffering, submission, derivative of Latin *passus,* past participle of *patī* to suffer, submit.[201]

- **Zest** [zest] *Origin*: 1665–75; < French *zest* (now *zeste*) orange or lemon peel used for flavoring.[202] I believe it is when you add flavor to something, to make it more exciting.

The Language of Winners!

— • —

JOHN R. NOE, IN HIS BOOK *Peak Performance Principles for High Achievers*, affirms, "True enthusiasm comes from giving ourselves to a purpose. High achievers have a purpose, and they have the heart to pursue it when other people quit."[203] This is true when you are passionate about winning; when you simply cannot wait for the sun to rise again so that you can get back to work on what makes your blood gush with emotion. That is the essence of zest – it will take your imagination by storm.

With a storm comes thunder and lightning; the lightning is your enthusiasm. You must allow it to strike again and again; capture it in a bottle if you can, and unleash it continuously on your goals, on your purpose, on your reason for being. You must constantly generate new enthusiasm, but you must also *maintain* it. Edward B. Butler said, "One man has enthusiasm for 30 minutes, another for 30 days, but it is the man who has it for 30 years who makes a success of his life."

In July 2005, after I returned victorious from the World Organization of Martial Arts Athletes (WOMAA) World Games VI in Rosenheim, Germany, I wore my Grand Championship ring to my medical clinic with a smile one day. I had won other World Championships before, but this was my very first

Champion of Champions award (i.e., the champion of the eleven male world championship divisions from the eighteen countries represented). I remember vividly when an elderly patient, Joaquin Gonzalez, asked, "Oiga doctorsito, ¿cuanto le costó ese anillo?" (Translation: "Hey Doc, how much did that ring cost?") My vibrant response was, "Mr. Gonzalez, ¡me costó 30 años!" ("Mr. Gonzalez, it cost me 30 years!") He nodded his head in pleasant surprise that I did not answer in dollars, but in time and effort. Dedicated work, passion, and perseverance allowed this world title to come home with me. However, I always like to say that the spirit of the Lord guided me toward this triumph – even before I understood what the origins of the words "enthusiasm" and "passion" meant!

This world championship ring is a palpable form of recognition for incessant dedication and hard work, which in turn fuels additional motivation for continued excellence. Zig Ziglar says, "the cheapest and most effective motivation in the marketplace is simple but sincere recognition for extra effort."[204] In fact, a recent study[205] showed that 65% of managers erroneously believed that money was the primary motivator of employee performance – boy, did the managers have it all wrong! Employees want to feel appreciated; they want to feel like what they do matters.

Thus, besides the phrases "thank you," "way to go," "keep up the great work," or "you're doing an awesome job," there is also the *say*, *see*, *feel* method of immediate, on-the-spot recognition. For example, "Mary, a lot of the staff is *saying* that you came up with some creative ideas for this project... congratulations!" or "Luis, I *see* your numbers are up this month... thanks for your dedication!" or "Nancy, I'm very *excited* that you had a successful booth at the conference this weekend!"

Without a doubt, words of encouragement will go a long way towards making the workplace a more enjoyable place to be, especially on Monday mornings and Friday afternoons. Employees yearn for appreciation and they have spoken. Specifically, here are some of the salient findings from another study, the 2011 Globoforce Workforce Mood Tracker Survey:[206]

- 85% of U.S. workers like to have their efforts recognized.
- 52% are dissatisfied with the level of recognition they receive for doing good work.
- 39% don't feel appreciated at their jobs.
- 53% don't believe their company cares about them.
- 78% of U.S. workers said that being recognized motivates them at their job.
- 69% said they'd work harder if they felt their efforts were better appreciated.

Taking these findings into account, Socialcast, a San Francisco-based maker of business software, gives five recommendations on how to better recognize employees for enhanced engagement and motivation.[207] Of course, this translates to a better work environment, improved work efficiency, greater loyalty, and superior production and results. And to better remember these strategies, I have created the acronym MERIT because winners *deserve a reward*.

M	=	**M**anipulation is a no-no; don't play favorites. You must justify nominations with fair and unbiased reasons.
E	=	**E**valuate criteria for rewards in a specific, clear, and consistent manner so everyone can strive for them and know what to expect.
R	=	**R**einforce recognition with follow-ups when improvements are noticed.
I	=	**I**dentity of those receiving the acknowledgment and the reasons why they were chosen should be crystal clear to everyone.
T	=	**T**iming is critical; reward quickly so that everyone understands the direct association of the recognition.

If done right, the *timing* of the MERIT approach can elevate and maintain the enthusiasm of the team for an extended time frame; if done wrong, it can quickly deflate the momentum that was building. In the business arena, I have witnessed team members accomplish a certain goal at the beginning of the month, only to be recognized in a 3-5 minute announcement in front of the cohort 28 to 30 days later. Sadly enough by then, the achiever felt unappreciated, the excitement of achieving the milestone had waned, and most people had forgotten why this person was being celebrated in the first place. Yes, timing *is* critical.

Indeed, it is difficult to maintain enthusiasm and motivation for a prolonged period of time. Daniel Pink, in the March 2011 *SUCCESS* CD, says there are three things that provide enduring motivation, both in business and in our personal lives:[208] 1) *Autonomy* – a sense of self-direction whereby you can engage in your work by having flexibility and freedom to guide your actions and to be creative, 2) *Mastery* – your desire to improve and to get better at your work or craft, and to get recognized for your achievements, and 3) *Purpose* – you get better results when you have a sense of purpose, when you know *why* you are doing what you are doing, instead of only knowing *how* to do it.

In *The HELP Secret*, I recommend that you write down your "why" early on when you start any venture.[209] You must be clear about what motivates you and inspires you. "It's important you have a strong sense of why you're doing this – "

I write, " – that way, when the going gets tough, you'll remember the exact circumstances that make you passionate about following your dreams."[210]

Autonomy, mastery, and a sense of purpose are undeniably very powerful long-term motivators; they will keep you enthusiastic for years. For some winners, *purpose* seems to be the strongest of the three. In fact, a catchy phrase that accentuates the magnitude of this element goes something like this: *If your why don't make you cry, it ain't gonna fly!*

On the other hand, short-term motivation and enthusiasm can die very quickly… unless it "catches on." I like to think of it as a medical analogy because in actuality, enthusiasm is like a communicable disease – it is highly contagious! And as it spreads from person to person, it gains momentum. Momentum fuels confidence which in turn leads to persistence, and persistence is a powerful element of winning. Winning will lead to more winning, and then it will become a habit. And once you have developed a winning habit, there is no stopping you and your dreams!

On March 6th of this year, I met a young man with a dream – Mauricio "Tony" Becerra. Tony is a winning poet, a motivational speaker, and one of the original *Freedom Writers* from Erin Gruwell's freshman English class.[211] That day in Eagle Pass, Texas, he recited some poetry while sharing his story of triumph over poverty, gang violence, an alcoholic father, and discrimination. During lunch, I asked if he would give me a few words for The *Language of Winners!* and he instinctively verbalized that poetry is his passion and that he volunteers as a Poetry teacher with underprivileged kids in California. He said that he loves to awaken the poet from within his students with simple exercises. For example, instead of saying, "Today is a good day!" – he recites an alternative phrase such as, "I utterly rejoice at the glorious rays of the sun as they rest upon my shoulders!" I was fascinated listening to his vocal rhythm, as I hurriedly transcribed his words. We went back to eating, but it was obvious that poetry pulsates through his body as blood circulates through his arteries. And that passion, that zest for words...for life, is what makes Tony Becerra a winner.

In *Success for Dummies*, Zig Ziglar says, "Check the records: Whether it's in music, medicine, physics, science, academics, or athletics, the great ones have passion for what they're doing."[212] But how do you develop your passion, your zest for life? Zig describes three steps[213] that are certain to assist you in developing your passion – I call them the ABCs:

Analyze what you want in life and formulate a plan for reaching your goals – and when the plan makes sense to you, you can commit to moving forward.

Begin the action steps toward your goals. Zig says it this way:[214]

As your plans unfold, each step that you take toward your goals has a direct bearing on your excitement, enthusiasm, and confidence. As you enjoy little successes, your imagination...explodes, and passion enters the picture. And when passion is full-blown, it's unlikely that you will abandon your objectives.

<u>C</u>ognition – use your head to guide your developing passion. Yes, many people refer to passion as having "heart" because passionate individuals seem to accomplish much more than what is possible via mental and/or physical abilities alone. However, it is cognition, your mental attributes and your knowledge, which bring that passion into focus to create a platform for your imagination to allow your heart to take you to the Promised Land.

Winners rejoice with enthusiasm and passion at the glory of each day because they have a compelling purpose and a clearly defined plan to get them to victory. Winners understand that besides lightning in a bottle, you need direction and longevity of your enthusiasm. Charles M. Schwab says, "A man can succeed at almost anything for which he has unlimited enthusiasm." As leaders, winners can continue to support and fuel enthusiasm into the team. Winners believe the main component in passion is your heart, but the guiding force for such energy is your head. Winners embrace the MERIT approach and recognize achievers in a timely fashion. And as a winner, you will infuse renewed enthusiasm to each of your team members by providing them supplementary guidance and inspiration with a copy of...*The Language of Winners!*

Epilogue –

When I examine myself and my methods of thought, I come to the conclusion that the gift of fantasy has meant more to me than any talent for abstract, positive thinking.
~ Albert Einstein

Epilogue [ep-uh-lawg, -log] *Origin*: 1564, from M.Fr. epilogue, from L. epilogus, from Gk. epilogos "conclusion of a speech," from epi- "upon, in addition" + logos "a speaking." Earliest Eng. sense was theatrical.[215]

- • -

CONGRATULATIONS – YOU'VE DONE IT! You are one of the few; you are amongst a small sub-set of the population; you have read a book that was not required for work or school![216] (Unless, of course, some crazy CEO from corporate America or an eccentric Professor at a liberal college or university includes it on their Required Reading list.) Notwithstanding this, perhaps after you have turned the last page and stopped to contemplate either a particular lesson learned or an *Aha! moment* from one of the many winners contained herein, you will undoubtedly face several options:

1. You can read, study, underline, circle, highlight, draw an arrow, put a check mark, dog ear, post-it note, or squiggly line this book again, as many times as your heart desires, and continue learning, being inspired, and improving your life and that of your loved ones.

2. You can put it away somewhere and risk never finding it again. Thus, transforming it into a hidden treasure for somebody to discover in a later generation.

3. You can give it to someone you care for (if you liked the book) or give it to someone you don't care for (if you didn't like the book).

4. You can sell it, trade it, or donate it to charity.

5. You can throw it away. The legendary Bruce Lee believed that you should keep what is useful and throw away the rest. If you have started your wind up and you are ready to toss this book into oblivion, I only ask one thing: Yes, throw it away – but throw it into the middle of the ocean, onto your sea of knowledge, so that it may start a ripple effect and positively influence the masses, many of whom you will never know. If you do not believe me, then simply toss the book into the nearest

trash container…but on the chance that you *do* believe, then options #1 and #5 are your best choices.

By sharing with you a personal story, I believe you will find it easier to decide which number you will select from the above list. But first, if you have not read a lot of books lately, do not despair – you *did* finish this one. And what a way to start your new library!

I have a passion for learning, reading, writing, and for sharing what I've learned. But reading and writing were not always this much fun for me. My reading acumen was way below par when I got to Brown University in 1976. In fact, I was not even accustomed to speaking the English language for any significant period of time – say, for more than 3 or 4 sentences in a row. Yes, I went to high school in south Texas, but Spanish seemed to be omnipresent with students *and* teachers, and my parents were Spanish-only monolinguals.

And so, arriving at an Ivy League institution and already behind – *way* behind – in oral communication skills and in overall knowledge only meant one thing: I had to work that much harder than everyone else *just to trail behind*. I remember the May 2011 issue of *SUCCESS magazine*, in which Darren Hardy says, "While I may be communicating with tens of thousands of people every day…I am not really connecting or fostering very many real relationships at all. I'm what's called a mile wide and an inch deep, and that's not how you strike oil!"[217]

If the idea is to strike oil, to strike it rich, to become successful, and to win at the game of life... I'm in – are you? And what Darren is saying is that if you are doing too many non-productive things that do not enhance your personal improvement (e.g., watching TV, surfing the internet, spending countless hours on Facebook, texting while driving, tweeting yourself to sleep, basically...going a mile wide) and not enough time dedicated to reading empowering books, to listening to inspirational audio programs, to attending personal development seminars (i.e., your knowledge base is shallow; you're an inch deep), then you will not succeed. So, the plan is to focus your energies on going deep by continually learning...and then you can strike oil.

Well, at Brown I was an inch wide and an inch deep – I needed lots of help. In my classes, everyone (professors and students) spoke at a much higher level than me. It took me only a few minutes to realize I had huge gaps in my learning; I did not understand most of what was being said! So I purchased a dictionary and I carried it everywhere with me. And whenever I read a word I was unfamiliar with, I drew a squiggly line under it – that was my signal to look it up. Other markings[218] – arrows, circles, rectangles, check marks, straight underlines, highlights, and dog eared pages – meant different things. I was now an active reader; I was surrounding myself with possibilities. And whenever I heard a word I did not know, I wrote it down and looked it up as soon as I could. As you can imagine, my textbooks were full of squiggly lines; as for my dictionary... I certainly got my money's worth.

The years passed, my knowledge base grew, my vocabulary improved, my oral communication skills flourished, my confidence followed an exponential curve, and the future was suddenly full of opportunities. And then it was time to go to medical school, and it was *déjà vu* all over again (I know it is redundant, but it sounds cool). I was way behind. I did not understand much of the medical terminology. But I knew what to do; I had a system – and yes, besides all my textbooks, I now carried with me *two* dictionaries – my dictionary from Brown and my medical dictionary. Markings and squiggly lines continued...and they continue to this day.

So, I reiterate: do not worry, do not despair. There is hope for a better tomorrow because you are taking the action steps today to secure your future. The hard part is over; you have taken that first step. All you have to do is keep going, stay on track, and if you go off on a tangent, remember to refocus and correct your course so you can continue moving forward. Above all, do not quit because *The Future is Now!* (my new slogan).

And if there is a word here or there that you do not understand, just look it up – but *look it up* because that way you will remember it better than if you ask someone to tell you the definition. Be an active learner, not a passive one. If you are not used to sitting and reading, that's okay too – start with ten minutes per day. Do that for a week, and then you can increase your time to 15 minutes a day for another week. After one month, you should be up to 30 minutes a day – and that's awesome! Do you realize that if you only read 30 minutes a day for one year, which is not very difficult, you would have read more than 25 books![219] Imagine the kind of person you would become, the kind of success you can achieve, the numerous opportunities you can attract, the type of fulfillment you will experience! Yes, you can do this – and you can encourage young people in your family to do this.

Give someone a book – any book, as long as it enhances their life and it's uplifting, it's positive, it's got a few words in Spanish (okay, that's not mandatory), it's educational and inspirational – and watch their world open up because *you* cared enough to give them this wonderful blessing. And remember that "a blessing is not a blessing until you speak it," according to Joel Osteen.[220] So, say something like, "Mary, I just finished reading this amazing book and I thought of you. You deserve an autographed copy, so here it is. I hope you enjoy it."

In conclusion, I would love to leave you with two things: a poem and a quote. The poem is first. I was inspired to write it while I was working on this book. I hope you enjoy its rhythm and its message.

The Language of Winners! – A Poem

A seed was planted in your mind,
   Of possibility and hope,
That words and actions must combine,
   To deal successfully – not mope.

You nurtured it with books galore;
   Triumphant you began this quest.
And as the seed began to soar,
   You soon found out that you were blessed.

Beyond the victories – you yearned,
   To spread the blessings and forgive.
The seasons passed and then you learned,
   Through selfless acts you start to live.

You were transformed – you will attest.
   Likewise, your worries were no more.
You speak the language of the best:
   Success will walk you through the door.

And finally, enjoy this quote from Virginia Woolf:[221]

> *I have sometimes dreamt, at least, that when the Day of Judgment dawns and the great conquerors and lawyers and statesmen come to receive their rewards – their crowns, their laurels, their names carved indelibly upon imperishable marble – the Almighty*

> *will turn to Peter and will say, not without a certain envy when he sees us coming with our books under our arms, "Look, these need no reward. We have nothing to give them here. They have loved reading."*

God bless you as you speak **The Language of Winners!** – now go out there and bless others. They deserve it...and *you* deserve it!

WINNERS –

I failed to make the chess team because of my height.
～ Woody Allen

Winners [win-ers] *Origin*: 1325-75, fusion of O.E. winnan "struggle for, work at, strive, fight," and gewinnan "to gain or succeed by struggling, to win," both from P.Gmc. *wenwanan (cf. O.S. winnan, O.N. vinna, O.Fris. winna, Du. winnen "to gain, win," Dan. vinde "to win," O.H.G. winnan "to strive, struggle, fight," Ger. gewinnen "to gain, win," Goth. gawinnen "to suffer, toil"). Perhaps related to wish, or from PIE *van- "overcome, conquer." Sense of "to be victorious" is recorded from c.1300. The noun in O.E. meant "labor, strife, conflict;" modern sense of "a victory in a game or contest" is first attested 1862, from the verb. Breadwinner (see bread) preserves the sense of "toil" in O.E. winnan. Phrase you can't win them all (1954) first attested in Raymond Chandler.[222]

- • -

THIS ALPHABETICAL LIST OF SUCCESSFUL INDIVIDUALS is designed to provide a brief description of some of their many accolades. They are winners who contributed a tiny portion of their vast wisdom into the creation of this book – and for that, I thank them and acknowledge their contributions. And unlike Woody Allen's quote above (I'm sure he's talking about the lack of height in his chess skills), all those listed here made the team – they had the height, the *stature* that is required to speak...***The Language of Winners!***

Abdel Kader – (1808-1883) An Algerian Islamic scholar, political and military leader who led a struggle against the French invasion in the mid-nineteenth century. For this, he is seen by some Algerians as their national hero.[223] He also practiced Sufism, through which one can know how to travel into the presence of the Divine, purify one's inner self from filth, and beautify it with a variety of praiseworthy traits.[224]

Abraham Lincoln – (1809-1865) The 16th President of the United States, he successfully led the USA through the American Civil War, preserving the Union, while ending slavery, and promoting economic and financial modernization. Mostly self-educated, he became a country lawyer and overcame many failures prior to being elected President.[225]

Alan Bates – (born 1945) An osteopathic doctor and Oregon State Senator.[226] He referenced the Pareto Principle in a debate on the floor of the State Senate in early 2012.

Albert Einstein – (1879-1955) German-born physicist who discovered the Theory of Relativity, within which the famous equation e=mc2 helped to unlock some of the mysteries of the Universe.[227]

Albert Mehrabian – (born 1939) Iranian-born Professor Emeritus of Psychology at UCLA. He is best known for his publications regarding verbal and nonverbal communication.[228]

Alex Leal – (unknown) After 31 seasons as head football coach in the Rio Grande Valley of south Texas, Coach Leal retired on December 2010 as the winningest coach in RGV history. Coach Leal gave me an opportunity to serve in my first Team Doctor "gig" for the McAllen High School Football Bulldogs.[229]

Alexis Liset Hinojosa – (known, but won't tell) My youngest child, Alexis or "Lexi" is an intelligent young lady who sings like an Angel. Okay, she was born in 1993 and she has a bright future ahead of her.

Anne Huber – (unknown) Ms. Huber was my *Personal and Reflective Writing* instructor at Brown University during my senior year (spring of 1980). Actually, the class was a freshman English class and I had not realized that I was lacking an English semester in order to graduate. I was already accepted into the University of Cincinnati College of Medicine but I still needed to take that English class my last semester at Brown...and I loved it! I credit Ms. Huber and that English class for igniting my writing passion. Thank you!

Aristotle – (384-322 BC) A Greek philosopher, student of Plato and teacher of Alexander the Great, Aristotle is one of the top 3 most important founding figures in Western philosophy. His writings were the first to create a comprehensive system of Western philosophy, including morality and aesthetics, logic and science, and politics and metaphysics.[230]

Austin Madison – (unknown) A Pixar animator, Austin graduated from the character animation program at California Institute of the Arts before landing his Pixar job.[231] He hand-wrote that wonderful letter of encouragement found in Chapter 16 – Patience, Part II.

Beatles, The – One of the most famous rock bands of all time, The Beatles were formed in Liverpool, England in 1960 and consisted of John Lennon, Paul McCartney, George Harrison, and Ringo Starr.[232]

Ben Parker – Fictional character that originally appeared in the 2002 *Spider-Man* film, where he uttered the famous line, "With great power comes great responsibility." Actor Cliff Robertson played the role of Ben Parker, also known as "Uncle Ben."[233]

Benjamin Franklin – (1706-1790) One of the Founding Fathers of the United States, Franklin was a leading author, printer, political theorist, politician, postmaster, scientist, musician, inventor, and diplomat. A major figure for his discoveries and theories regarding electricity, he also invented bifocals and formed the first public lending library in America and the first fire department in Pennsylvania.[234]

Brian Tracy – (born 1944) A Canadian-born self-help author and motivational speaker. One of the legends in the Personal Improvement industry.[235] Brian Tracy has written and produced more than 500 audio and video learning programs, authored more than 50 books on leadership, selling, self-esteem, goals and more; this translates to more than one book or program per month consistently for 30 consecutive years![236]

Bruce Lee – (1940-1973) Born Lee Jun-fan in San Francisco to parents of Hong Kong heritage, Bruce was raised in Hong

Kong until his late teens. Bruce Lee is regarded by many as the most famous martial arts movie actor of all time. In addition, he was a martial arts instructor, philosopher, film director, film producer, screenwriter, and founder of the Jeet Kune Do martial arts movement.[237]

C.C. Bloom – Fictional character that appeared in the 1988 film *Beaches*, where she uttered the great line, "But enough about me, let's talk about you – what do YOU think about me?" Actress Bette Midler played the role of C.C. Bloom.[238]

Charles M. Schwab – (1862-1939) An American steel magnate, not to be confused with Charles R. Schwab, the businessman/philanthropist founder and chairman of Charles Schwab Corporation.[239]

Chris Widener – (unknown) An internationally recognized speaker since 1988, Chris is also an author (he co-wrote *Twelve Pillars* with Jim Rohn) and radio host. He founded the Personal Development website MadeForSuccess.com.[240]

Cyril Northcote Parkinson – (1909-1993) A British naval historian and author of about sixty books, the most famous of which was the bestseller *Parkinson's Law*, for which he is considered an important scholar within the field of public administration.[241]

Dale Carnegie – (1888-1955) An American writer, lecturer, and developer of famous courses on personal development, selling, corporate training, public speaking, and interpersonal skills. He authored the bestseller *How to Win Friends and Influence People* (1936), which remains popular today, as evidenced by the fact that I quoted it on Chapter 6 – Focus.[242]

Daniel Levitin, PhD – (born 1957) A prominent cognitive psychologist, neuroscientist, record producer, musician, and writer. He teaches Psychology, Behavioral Neuroscience, Music Theory, Computer Science, and Education at McGill University in Montreal, Quebec, Canada.[243]

Daniel Paisner – (unknown) Co-authored *The Brand Within* with Daymond John. His website includes the following quote on the home page: author... "ghost-writer"... reasonably nice guy...tall for his age..."[244] This pretty much says it all.

Daniel Pink – (unknown) An American author and journalist, Daniel Pink was the chief speechwriter for Vice-President Al Gore. He has written four best-sellers, with his most recent work entitled *Drive: The Surprising Truth About What Motivates Us*.[245]

Darren Hardy – (unknown, but he's young and energetic) As the publisher of *SUCCESS magazine,* Darren gets to engage with and interview the world's leading experts on human performance and achievement, some of the top CEOs, innovative entrepreneurs, star athletes, and other winners, to reveal and share their success secrets each and every month. I've quoted Darren and his work throughout this book so much that it behooves you to look further into what he's doing. He also authored *The Compound Effect*, which is also quoted herein. Lastly, as a subscriber of *SUCCESS magazine*, I find that the audio CD program contained within each issue is extremely valuable, as evidenced by the fact that I quoted many of the audio interviews in this book.[246] I've also heard Darren as a public speaker, and he's simply phenomenal.

David Brinkley – (1920-2003) An American TV newscaster from 1943 to 1997 and author of the critically acclaimed 1988 bestseller *Washington Goes to War*.[247]

David H. Song, MD – (unknown) An internationally recognized expert in Plastic Surgery, Dr. Song is the Chief of Plastic and Reconstructive Surgery at the University of Chicago Medical Center. He is fluent in Korean and English and provides free surgical care for children with congenital deformities in the Dominican Republic.[248]

Daymond John – (born 1969) An American entrepreneur, investor, TV personality (appears on the ABC show *Shark Tank*), author (he co-authored *The Brand Within* with Daniel Paisner) and motivational speaker. He is founder, president, and CEO of FUBU.[249] In his Wikipedia profile, there is a photo of Daymond speaking at a national convention in Dallas – I was there and Daymond did a phenomenal job!

Diana Lopez – (born 1984) An American-born Tae Kwon Do practitioner of Nicaraguan descent. Diana is a world champion and an Olympian, having represented the USA in the 2008 Beijing Olympics. In 2005, Diana and her brothers, Steven and Mark, made history by becoming the first three siblings *in any sport* to win World Championships at the same event during the World Tae Kwon Do Championships in Madrid, Spain.[250] Congrats, to the Lopez' siblings!

Dr. Jack Stanley, PhD – (unknown, but still going strong) The Theatre-TV-Film coordinator at the University of Texas-Pan American in Edinburg, Texas, Dr. Stanley is a professor, director, author, and actor.[251] I have taken several classes with Dr. Stanley and have shared the stage in a number of theatrical productions with him – thank you. In the photo that appears in the university website profile of Dr. Stanley, I noticed he has stepped out of his comfort zone and has started to wear other colors. Well done!

Earl Nightingale – (1921-1989) An American motivational speaker and author, Nightingale was known as the "Dean of Personal Development," and did voice over work in the 1950s and was a radio show host from 1950 to 1956. As an author, he wrote *The Strangest Secret*, which was called "...one of the great motivational books of all time" by economist Terry Savage.[252]

Edward B. Butler – (1853-1928) An American businessman who founded Butler Brothers department stores.[253] "Mr. Butler was representative of that rare race of men in whom greatness is simplicity, sympathy, modesty and almost superhuman ability."[254]

Edward James Olmos – (born February 24, 1947) An American-born actor and director of Mexican descent.[255] He has done a superb job in many films, but the one that captivated me was *Stand and Deliver*, where he portrays math teacher Jaime Escalante. Mr. Olmos and I share the same birth day, different year – brilliant!

Eleanor Roosevelt – (1884-1962) As the First Lady for the United States (1933-1945), Eleanor Roosevelt supported the New Deal policies of her husband, President Franklin D. Roosevelt. She became an advocate for civil rights and was an international author and speaker after her husband's death in 1945.[256]

Elisa "Licha" Fernández – One of my mother's older sisters, whom I used to call "Tia Licha." She was a visionary of sorts and had great energy.

Epictetus – (AD 55 - AD 135) A Greek sage and philosopher who believed philosophy was a way of life and not just a theoretical discipline.[257]

Eric Lee – (unknown, but still kicking) First and foremost, Eric Lee is a wonderful human being and I am proud to call him my close friend. He is a film actor, world champion martial artist, author, hall of famer, mentor, and budding comedian and musician. It was in his car that I physically began writing my book *Master and Disciple*! My children love him and so do I – thank you, my friend. Please check out his website www.EricLee.com to get a glimpse of everything he does.

Erin Gruwell – (born 1969) An American English teacher who inspired underprivileged and gang-influenced students to overcome their obstacles. Her unorthodox teaching method led to the publication of the book *The Freedom Writers Diary: How a Teacher and 150 Teens Used Writing to Change Themselves and the World Around Them* (1999) and later the film *Freedom Writers* (2007), starring Hillary Swank.[258]

Ernest Buffett – (1877-1946) Grandfather of one of the wealthiest men in the world, Warren Buffett. Ernest Buffett, a grocery store manager, shared some time-tested advice with his children in the form of a letter which is transcribed in Chapter 8 – Habits.[259]

Erwin Smigel – (unknown) Author of *The Wall Street Lawyer: Professional Organization Man?* published in 1969.[260]

F. Scott Fitzgerald – (1896-1940) Author of *The Great Gatsby*, a work that seriously examines the theme of aspiration in an American setting and defines the classic American novel. A University of South Carolina website states that "the dominant influences on F. Scott Fitzgerald were aspiration, literature, Princeton, Zelda Sayre Fitzgerald, and alcohol."[261]

Freddy Peralta – (born 1955) Originally from the Dominican Republic, Freddy is a close friend who started out as one of my patients when I was a practicing family physician in south Texas. In fact, Freddy considers it a great honor that he was the last patient seen by me prior to my retirement in early 2010 – ditto for me. Freddy Peralta is a successful business owner, entrepreneur, team leader, and a very eloquent Spanish professional speaker and Master of Ceremonies. Thank you for your friendship, Freddy.

Harvey Mackay – (born 1932) An American-born businessman, author, professional speaker, and columnist, Harvey Mackay is best known for his best-sellers, including Swim With the Sharks (Without Being Eaten Alive), among others. He is also founder, chairman, and CEO of Mackay Envelope Corporation.[262]

Henry F. Cope – (1870-1923) Born in London, England, Henry F. Cope was a major figure in the rise of the Religious Education Movement. He is best remembered for his service as general secretary of the Religious Education Association from 1907 until his death in 1923. He wrote a number of books regarding religious education.[263]

Henry Ford – (1863-1947) An American industrialist, the founder of the Ford Motor Company, and sponsor of the development of the assembly line technique of mass production. His Model T automobile revolutionized transportation and American industry, and he became one of the wealthiest and best-known individuals in the world.[264]

Henry Russell "Red" Sanders – (1905-1958) An American football player and coach, Red Sanders was head coach at Vanderbilt University and UCLA. Coach Sanders was inducted into the College Football Hall of Fame as a coach in 1996. He is credited with coining the phrase, "Winning isn't everything; it's the only thing" and when asked about the UCLA-USC rivalry, he said, "It's not a matter of life and death, it's more important than that!"[265]

Homero Hinojosa – (born 1924) My father; the oldest of five children born to Luis Hinojosa and Faustina Guerra in General Treviño, Nuevo León, México. He is credited with coining the phrase, "¡Ay, mi'jo – tú miras bien alto y tu padre está bien chaparro!" in response to when, at the age of 5 years, I said aloud that I wanted to become a doctor when I grow up. (Translation: "Ah, son – you aim so tall and your father is so short!")

Hong Kang Kim – (unknown) My Grand Master in Tae Kwon Do, from Cincinnati, Ohio. When I started medical school in 1980, I made a decision to focus *only* in my studies - mistake. And since I was already a Black Belt in Tae Kwon Do, I sadly put it on the back burner for the first trimester (10 weeks). Unfortunately, although I was "always at the library," my grades suffered. When I met with Dean Norma Wagoner to figure out why I wasn't excelling in medical school, she asked that I describe a typical day for me at Brown. She instantly identified my deficiency and ordered, "I want you to walk out that door and find yourself a Tae Kwon Do school!" She did not have to tell me twice. I got on my car and drove around Cincinnati until 9:55pm, when I stopped at GM Kim's school. The gentle Korean man was locking up for the evening as I arrived. He smiled and asked in a calm, yet powerful tone, "May I help you?" and I was hooked – similar to the phrase, "You had me at hello," from the *Jerry McGuire* film. And my grades in med school quickly recovered; and even my roommate, Frank LoRusso, and other classmates commented on my dramatic improvement. Thank you, Grand Master Kim!

Hunter Kelly – (1997-2005) Son of football legend Jim Kelly and his wife, Jill. Hunter was given no more than a few years to live after being diagnosed with Krabbe Disease, a fatal nervous system disease, but he fought it for eight years! Jim and Jill started the Hunter's Hope Foundation in 1997, in honor of their son. Currently, the disease has no known cure, but many families have been positively affected by the Foundation.[266]

Isabel Gauthier, PhD – (born 1971) A Canadian-born cognitive neuroscientist that currently holds the position of professor and head of the Object Perception Lab at Vanderbilt University's Department of Psychology. Her work mainly focuses on the role of perception in domains such as faces, letters, or musical notation.[267]

Jackie Chan – (born 1954) Born in Hong Kong, he was named Chan Kong-sang, or "born in Hong Kong." Jackie Chan is a world-renowned film superstar who does his own stunts; he is also a martial artist and funny man.[268] He made a special personal appearance when I accompanied our USA Team to the 1997 World Tae Kwon Do Championships in Hong Kong. As soon as he took the stage, there was pandemonium! For obvious security reasons, Jackie was quickly taken off the stage. I'll meet you next time, Jackie, next time...

Jaime Escalante – (1930-2010) A Bolivian educator, Escalante taught calculus at Garfield High School, East Los Angeles, California from 1974 to 1991. He was the subject of the 1988 film *Stand and Deliver*, in which Edward James Olmos portrays Escalante.[269]

James B. Hall, PhD – (unknown) Dr. Hall was my Neuro Anatomy and Gross Anatomy professor at the University of Cincinnati College of Medicine. One of my earliest encounters with him was on a Gross Anatomy oral/practical exam during my first year. Groups of four students at a time would walk to a table consisting of a cadaver with a bunch of tags on tiny anatomical areas of the body, and the professor would ask a series of questions. It was toward the end of the testing session and our body part was the head and neck area – lots of little arteries, veins, nerves, etc. It was my turn and I was to identify the area depicted by the tiny tag – it was underneath a bunch of complex structures in the neck area. After I gave my final answer (they didn't call it that in med school), Dr. Hall declared, "That's the first time today somebody gets it right!" Dr. Hall was one of the select few who honored me with writing a Letter of Recommendation for my Family Practice Residency Program. Thank you, Dr. Hall!

James R. Sherman, PhD – (unknown) Author of personal improvement books, including *Plan Your Work / Work Your Plan*.

Jawaharlal Nehru – (1889-1964) An Indian lawyer, politician and statesman who became the first Prime Minister of independent India (1947-1964). One of the principal leaders of India's independence movement in the 1930s and 1940s.[270]

Jean Lopez – (unknown) A Nicaraguan-born Tae Kwon Do practitioner, Jean is an elite competitor, but his claim to fame has been as US Olympic and World Championship coach. In 2005, Jean coached his three siblings (Diana, Steven, and Mark) to the three-peat Gold Medal performances where they made history by becoming the first three siblings *in any sport* to win World Championships at the same event during the World Tae Kwon Do Championships in Madrid, Spain.[271] Congrats again to the Lopez clan!

Jeff Olson – (unknown) An American-born personal improvement leader, Jeff founded *The People's Network*, a company that became one of the largest personal development training companies in America. Jeff authored *The Slight Edge* and the audio book, as well[272] – that's the one I have, and it's great!

Jeffrey Zaslow – (1958-2012) An American author, journalist, and columnist for *The Wall Street Journal*. He co-authored *The Last Lecture* with Randy Pausch. Tragedy struck Jeffrey in the form of a motor vehicle accident where he died while on a book tour for his book *The Magic Room*.[273]

Jerry Hardy – (unknown) The father of *SUCCESS magazine* publisher, Darren Hardy. As a football coach, Jerry Hardy's strict disciplinarian approach helped Darren become the personal improvement leader he is today.[274]

Jesus Rodriguez, MD – (unknown) My personal friend and mentor, Dr. Rodriguez is a formidable surgeon in south Texas with 59 years' experience who has operated on both of my parents, multiple times – that shows the kind of confidence I have in his skills. Always with a calm demeanor, Dr. Rodriguez may be heard whistling beautiful tunes while he saves lives in the Operating Room.[275]

Jill Kelly – (unknown) An author, speaker, child of God, mother, and wife of football legend Jim Kelly. Co-founded *Hunter's Hope Foundation* in honor of her son, Hunter, who passed away at the age of 8 due to an incurable neurological disorder.[276]

Jim Kelly – (born 1960) A former American football quarterback with the NFL's Buffalo Bills and the USFL's Houston Gamblers, Jim was inducted into the Pro Football Hall of Fame in 2002. He and his wife, Jill, co-founded

Hunter's Hope Foundation in honor of their son, Hunter, who passed away at the age of 8 due to an incurable neurological disorder.[277]

Jim Rohn – (1930-2009) An American entrepreneur, author, mentor, and motivational speaker, Jim's rags to riches story has influenced many in the personal development industry. Widely known as "America's foremost business philosopher," Jim Rohn died of Pulmonary Fibrosis in December 2009.[278] I believe Jim Rohn is one of my top mentors in the area of Personal Improvement. You are missed, Jim!

Jim Wagner – (unknown, but still kicking) A world-renowned expert in personal protection, Jim is a close friend of mine. We were roommates in the Aspen Academy of Martial Arts in 1978, when we trained under the legendary Dan Inosanto, Bruce Lee's best friend. Jim is founder of the Jim Wagner Reality-Based Personal Protection program, for which I am his Spanish language director. Jim has appeared on the cover of multiple martial arts magazines and is a hall of fame martial artist. Thanks for all you do, amigo![279]

José Luis "JL" Hinojosa, II – (born 1990) My first-born and favorite son – although he reminds me that he is my *only* son. JL has a sharp mind and effortless basketball moves. In fact, basketball is his passion and he is also being groomed as a public speaker. I rejoice at the positive future that lies in front of him.

Joaquin González – (born 1923) Mr. González was a patient when I was a practicing physician. He and his wife invited me to their home on several occasions. Spending that type of personal time with nice people has always been a great source of fulfillment for me. But I had to be careful with Mr.

González: if I gave him a compliment about his shirt or an accessory, I was afraid he would take it off and give it to me!

Joe Friday – A fictional character that was created and played by American actor, television producer, and writer Jack Webb (1920-1982) on the TV show Dragnet. The series ran on radio, TV, and there was even a theatrical film in 1954 and a TV movie in 1969.[280]

Joe Navarro – (born 1953) A Cuban-born author, public speaker, and ex-FBI agent and supervisor, Navarro specializes in non-verbal communication.[281]

Joel Osteen – (born in 1963) An American author, televangelist, and the senior pastor of Lakewood Church in Houston, Texas, Joel's ministry reaches millions of weekly viewers in over 100 countries around the world.[282] My wife and I attended Lakewood once and it was an unbelievable experience! Stop by if you're in the Houston area sometime.

Johann Kaspar Lavater – (1741-1801) A Swiss poet, Lavater also practiced physiognomy, the assessment of a person's character or personality from his outer appearance, especially the face.[283]

John Bunyan – (1628-1688) An English Christian writer and preacher, famous for writing *The Pilgrim's Progress*, but also wrote other works including *The Life and Death of Mr. Badman*,[284] which is cited in *The Language of Winners!*

John C. Maxwell – (born 1947) Widely known as America's foremost authority on Leadership, Maxwell is an evangelical Christian author, speaker, and pastor who has written over 60 books, mainly on Leadership.[285] I've listened to John Maxwell's audio programs so much that I believe he is one of my top 3 mentors on Leadership.

John D. Rockefeller – (1839-1937) An American oil industrialist, investor, and philanthropist, John Davison Rockefeller founded the Standard Oil Company in 1870. As kerosene and gasoline grew in importance, his wealth increased until he became the world's richest man and the first American to be worth than 1 billion dollars. He is often considered to be the richest person in history![286]

John Donne – (1572-1631) An English poet, satirist, lawyer, and priest, Donne is considered the pre-eminent ambassador of the metaphysical poets.[287]

John F. Kennedy – (1917-1963) John Fitzgerald "Jack" Kennedy, also known as JFK, was the 35th President of the United States, serving from 1961 until his assassination in 1963. Today, he continues to rank highly in public opinion ratings of former US presidents.[288] His son, John Jr., was a freshman at Brown when I was a senior – and when the media outlets asked him why he selected Brown when "all the Kennedys" went to Harvard, he simply said, "Brown is better!"

John Grisham – (born 1955) An American lawyer and best-selling author, Grisham is best known for his legal thrillers. *The Firm* was his first best-seller,[289] but *The Testament* has some excellent dialogue, some of which was quoted in *The Language of Winners!*

John Guare – (born 1938) An American playwright, Guare is best known for *The House of Blue Leaves*, *Six Degrees of Separation*, and *Landscape of the Body*.[290] Some of the ideas from *Six Degrees of Separation* are echoed in *The Language of Winners!*

John Wooden – (1910-2010) An American basketball player and coach, Wooden was nicknamed the "Wizard of Westwood" because he won ten NCAA national championships within a

12-year period (including seven in a row!), as head coach at UCLA. He was the first person to ever be inducted into the Basketball Hall of Fame, both as a player and as a coach. Coach Wooden was also known, and loved, for his inspirational messages to his players, including his "Pyramid of Success" which gave sage advice not only for basketball success, but also for success in life.[291] My son, JL, loves Coach Wooden's book *Wooden: A Lifetime of Observations and Reflections On and Off the Court*, which he loaned me as a reference for *The Language of Winners!*

José Ardón – (unknown) The world's #1 Hispanic money earner in Network Marketing, José is from Honduras and now resides in Texas. He proudly announces that he finished his career in four years, but what he is really saying is that he only went up to the 4th grade in school and is now living the American Dream! He reminds people, "If I can do it, you can do it!" José is featured on the cover of *Success from Home* magazine (Year 8, No. 3, p32-33).

Jesus Marquez – (unknown) A two-time World Champion in Olympic style Tae Kwon Do, Marquez is from Spain and is the athlete who defeated Jean Lopez (from the USA) for the Gold Medal in the story you read about in Chapter 5 – Education, Part I.[292]

Juan Homero Hinojosa, PhD – (born 1957) My older brother, whom I love for many reasons. He walked in front, carrying a *machete*, and cleared the way for everyone from our family to pursue higher education. He went to Brown University first, and then inspired me to apply. He received his PhD in GeoPhysics from Johns Hopkins University in Baltimore, Maryland... and even discovered a new and improved method of measuring gravity!

Judith Orasanu – (unknown) With a PhD in Experimental Psychology, Dr. Orasanu works at NASA in the Systems Safety Research Branch, in California.[293] Some of her research findings regarding airplane captains and first officers is included in *The Language of Winners!*

Julius Caesar – (100-44 BC) As a Roman general and statesman, and writer of Latin prose, Caesar played a critical role in the transformation of the Roman Republic into the Roman Empire.[294]

Keith Vitali – (born 1952) Keith is an American-born martial artist, actor, producer, author, and child activist. He is a hall of fame martial artist and *Black Belt magazine* named him one of the ten best fighters of all time![295] Keith is my good friend and I was truly honored when he asked me to write the Foreword for his 2007 book *Bullyproof Your Child*. I look forward to his upcoming film on Daniel Boone's life, which I'm supposed to help out on – so, call me when you need me, Keith!

Kim Curby – (unknown) An Australian-born PhD in Psychology, Dr. Curby works at Temple University, where she focuses on visual learning – more specifically, face recognition, object recognition, and pattern recognition learning.[296]

Lao Tzu – (604 BC) Lao Tzu was a philosopher of ancient China and was best known as the author of the Tao Te Ching, which has led for him to be widely considered as the founder of philosophical Taoism (pronounced "Daoism").[297]

Laura Grisel Hinojosa – (born 1992) My second child, Laura or "Lori" is an intelligent young lady whose personality is very much like her dad's. Just like her two siblings, Laura always lights up my life and great things await her.

Les Brown – (born 1945) Leslie "Les" C. Brown is an American-born motivational speaker, speech coach, and best-selling author. He is considered one of the top motivational speakers anywhere.[298]

Lord Chesterfield – (1600s) Lord Chesterfield, or Earl of Chesterfield, was a title in the Peerage of England that was created in 1628 for Philip Stanhope, 1st Baron Stanhope.[299]

Lori Greiner – (unknown) An American inventor and entrepreneur, Lori is a well-known TV personality in programs such as QVC and, most recently, ABCs *Shark Tank*.[300]

Lou Ferrigno – (born 1951) Louis Jude "Lou" Ferrigno is an American actor, fitness trainer/consultant, author, and retired professional bodybuilder. He won Mr. Universe twice and is best known for portraying the lead role in the CBS TV series The Incredible Hulk from 1977 to 1981.[301]

Malcolm Gladwell – (born 1963) A Canadian-born journalist, best-selling author, and speaker, Gladwell has been a staff writer for *The New Yorker* since 1996. He has written four books, all of which have made it to the *New York Times* Bestsellers list.[302] His book *Outliers* is referenced in *The Language of Winners!*

Margarita "May" Hinojosa – (born 1965) My youngest sister, May is blessed with beauty and brains... plus a great attitude towards life. She received her Master's degree in Bilingual Education in Curriculum and Instruction, and loves teaching in San Antonio, Texas.

Maria Elena Hinojosa – (of course I can't reveal it here; my wife would kill me) My lovely wife who always supports me in my endeavors. I couldn't pen a book about winners without including her. Thank you, *mi amor*, for everything you represent.

Marian Monta, PhD – (unknown) A retired Professor and Artistic Director Emeritus of the University of Texas-Pan American University Theatre,[303] Dr. Monta was my first acting teacher. I played the part of Narrator and Mysterious Man for her Directorial Swan Song, *Into the Woods*, which turned out to be a wonderful experience. Dr. Monta was also my patient for a while.

Marianne Williamson – (born 1952) A best-selling author, spiritual activist, and lecturer, Marianne Williamson is founder of The Peace Alliance, a grassroots campaign supporting legislation to establish a United States Department of Peace.[304]

Mark Asher – (unknown) Author of the book *Body Language*, which was referenced in *The Language of Winners!*

Mark Cuban – (born 1958) The owner of the NBAs Dallas Mavericks, business magnate and investor with a background in computing and software, owner of Landmark Theatres and Magnolia Pictures, and the chairman of the HDTV cable network HDNet. In addition, Mark is a "shark" investor in the ABC show *Shark Tank* and authored a book in 2011 entitled *How to Win at the Sport of Business*.[305]

Mark Lopez – (born 1982) An American-born Tae Kwon Do practitioner of Nicaraguan descent. Mark is a world champion and an Olympian, having represented the USA in the 2008 Beijing Olympics. In 2005, Mark and his siblings, Steven and Diana, made history by becoming the first three siblings *in any sport* to win World Championships at the same event during the World Tae Kwon Do Championships in Madrid, Spain.[306] Congrats again, to the Lopez family!

Mark Twain – (1835-1910) As an American author and humorist, Mark Twain was his pen name; his real name was Samuel Langhorne Clemens. He is best known for his novels *The Adventures of Tom Sawyer* (1876) and its sequel, *Adventures of Huckleberry Finn* (1885); the Finn novel is often called "the Great American novel."[307]

Martin Luther King, Jr. – (1929-1968) An American clergyman, activist, Baptist minister, and prominent leader in the Civil Rights Movement for African-Americans. King is best known for his role in the advancement of civil rights not only in America, but throughout the world, by following the non-violent teachings of Mahatma Gandhi.[308]

Marvin Phillips – (unknown) A minister and author, Marvin Phillips "helps us laugh at ourselves, love others, and enjoy life the way God meant it to be."[309]

Michael Bernoff – (unknown) An American top performer in direct sales, a corporate recruiter, a professional speaker, and a sales trainer.[310]

Michael Jordan – (born 1963) A former American professional basketball player, entrepreneur, and majority owner of the Charlotte Bobcats NBA team, Michael Jordan is considered by many as the greatest basketball player of all time.[311]

Muhammad Ali – (born 1942) Born as Cassius Marcellus Clay, Jr., Ali is a former professional boxer, philanthropist, and social activist. He was World Heavyweight Champion three times, and proclaimed himself as "The Greatest."[312]

Napoleon Hill – (1883-1970) An American author and a legend in the field of Personal Success literature, Hill's most famous book, *Think and Grow Rich* (1937) is one of the best-selling books of all time.[313] As a teen, my mother gave me my very first book ever on Personal Improvement. It was a book in Spanish entitled *Piense y Hagase Rico* ("*Think and Grow Rich*") – what a gift!

Napoleon III – (1808-1873) Louis-Napoleon Bonaparte was the President of the French Second Republic. However, as the ruler of the Second French Empire, he was known as Napoleon III.[314]

Neil Armstrong – (born 1930) An American former astronaut, test pilot, aerospace engineer, University of Cincinnati professor, and the first person to set foot and walk on the Moon.[315]

Nelson Boswell – (unknown) Author of books on inner peace, success, and on nurturing loving relationships.[316]

Oprah Winfrey – (born 1954) An American media proprietor, talk show host, actress, producer and philanthropist, Oprah is best known for her TV talk show, which has become the highest-rated program of its kind in history. The show was nationally syndicated from 1986 to 2011. According to some assessments, she has been dubbed as the world's most influential woman.[317]

Pablo Picasso – (1881-1973) A Spanish painter, sculptor, printmaker, and stage designer, Picasso was one of the greatest and most influential artists of the 20th century. He is also known for co-inventing collage and for the wide variety of styles he helped develop and explore, among other things.[318]

Paul Zane Pilzer – (born 1954) A world-renowned economist, entrepreneur, adjunct professor, and best-selling author, Paul Zane Pilzer became Citibank's youngest vice president at age 26.[319]

Peter Bardatsos – (unknown) Panagiotis "Peter" Bardatsos is a former US Tae Kwon Do National team member and international competitor. He is currently on the USA National Team Coaching staff.[320] I had the pleasure of working with Peter during my years with the US National Tae Kwon Do team.

Peter Jackson – (born 1961) A New Zealand film director, producer, actor, and screenwriter, Peter is best known for his *The Lord of the Rings* film trilogy.[321]

Presley Swagerty – (born 1958?) A highly-sought out speaker, trainer, and motivator, Presley is an entrepreneur and the #1 money earner with one of the fastest growing companies in America. Known as "The Coach," Presley also authored his first book in 2012 entitled *Millionaire by Halftime*, published by Southpointe Publications.[322] (Go to MillionaireByHalftime.com to get your copy of Presley's wonderful book.) Presley is a good friend and inspiration – and thanks again for writing the Foreword for *The Language of Winners!* amigo.

Ralph Waldo Emerson – (1803-1882) An American essayist, lecturer, and poet, Emerson was a philosopher who led the Transcendentalist movement of the mid-19th century.[323]

Randy Pausch – (1960-2008) Randolph Frederick "Randy" Pausch was an American professor of computer science and human-computer interactions and design at Carnegie Mellon University. This fellow Brown alumnus learned that he had pancreatic cancer in 2006 and then gave a powerful lecture entitled "The Last Lecture: Really Achieving Your Childhood Dreams" in 2007, which gained him so much popularity on YouTube, that he later co-authored his book *The Last Lecture*, which became a best-seller.[324]

Robert Herjavec – (born 1963) Yugoslavian-born Canadian businessman, investor, and TV personality with the ABC show *Shark Tank*, Robert is currently the CEO of The Herjavec Group, a security software company.[325]

Robert Kiyosaki – (born 1947) Robert Toru Kiyosaki is an American author, motivational speaker, businessman, investor, and financial literacy activist. He is best known for the book Rich Dad Poor Dad, which expanded into a series, then into other self-help materials published and promoted under the Rich Dad brand.[326]

Roger Dawson – (unknown) An English-born professional speaker and trainer, Dawson is a well-known Power Negotiating expert.[327]

Ron White – (unkown) As one of the world's top memory experts, Ron White is a two time USA National memory champion.[328] He is simply amazing to watch and learn from!

Rosalinda Fernández de Hinojosa – (1931-2005) My mother; she was born in Villaldama, Nuevo León, Tamaulipas, México as the 9th child (out of 10) to Simon Fernández and Bethzabé Ramón. Among many things, she is credited with having the vision to bring her family to America, in search of a better future – despite dad's stubbornness not to want to.

Samson Raphael Hirsch – (1808-1888) A German rabbi best known as the intellectual founder of the *Torah im Derech Eretz* school of contemporary Orthodox Judaism.[329]

Stephen Covey – (born 1932) An American-born author and professor at Jon M. Huntsman School of Business at Utah State University, Stephen Covey's claim to fame is his best-selling book *The 7 Habits of Highly Effective People*.[330]

Stephen G. Post, PhD – (unknown) An internationally renowned author for his research and public speaking on benevolent and compassionate love at the interface of health, philanthropy, science and spirituality. Dr. Post is a best-selling author of the book *The Hidden Gifts of Helping: How the Power of Giving, Compassion, and Hope Can Get Us Through Hard Times*.[331]

Steve Jobs – (February 24, 1955-October 5, 2011) An American businessman, designer and inventor, Steven Paul "Steve" Jobs is best known as the co-founder, chairman, and CEO of Apple Inc. Jobs also co-founded Pixar Animation Studios and became a member of the board of directors of The Walt Disney Company in 2006, when Disney acquired Pixar. He died of complications from pancreatic cancer, which was diagnosed in 2003.[332]

Steven Lopez – (born 1978) Born in Nicaragua, Steven Lopez is an Olympian with 2 Gold medals and 1 Bronze in Tae Kwon Do. He is the first American fighter to win 5 World Championships.[333] Steven was in the Junior National Team when I was Team Doctor and we got to travel to international competitions together. Even then, before he suddenly grew, he was a joy to watch. Way to go, Steven!

Thomas Edison – (1847-1931) An American inventor and businessman, Thomas Alva Edison developed many devices that greatly influenced the entire world, including the phonograph, the motion picture camera, and a long-lasting, practical electric light bulb.[334]

Thomas H. Palmer – (1782-1861) An American educator, Thomas H. Palmer is best known for authoring The Teacher's Manual (1840), which includes the poem "Try, Try Again."[335]

Thomas à Kempis – (1380-1471) A German-born late Medieval Catholic monk and the likely author of The Imitation of Christ, one of the best known Christian books on devotion. His name means "Thomas of Kempen," his home town – and in German, he is known as Thomas von Kempen.[336]

Tom Hopkins – (unknown) Known as America's #1 Sales Trainer, Tom Hopkins is a professional speaker and trainer. His flagship program, How to Master the Art of Selling Anything, is widely used as a requirement for new salespeople by sales and management professionals in a wide variety of industries.[337]

Tony Becerra – (unknown) Mauricio "Tony" Becerra is a first generation American who grew up in poverty with an alcoholic father and busy mother. The frequent victim of bullying, Tony Becerra hated school and did poorly...until he met his new freshman English teacher, Ms. Erin Gruwell. Tony and the rest of Ms. Gruwell's class wrote the book *The Freedom Writers Diary*, which was later made into the major motion picture *Freedom Writers*, starring Hillary Swank.[338] Keep being an inspiration, Tony!

Tony Robbins – (born 1960) Anthony "Tony" Robbins is an American self-help author, peak performance coach, and motivational speaker. He became well known through his infomercials and books, Unlimited Power: The New Science of Personal Achievement and Awaken the Giant Within. His personal mentor was the great Jim Rohn.[339]

Ute Fischer, PhD – (unknown) Dr. Fischer is on the faculty at Georgia Institute of Technology, in the School of Literature,

Communication, and Culture. Her research has to do with team decision making in complex engineered environments, such as commercial aviation and space missions.[340]

Vilfredo Pareto – (1848-1923) Vilfredo Federico Damaso Pareto was an Italian engineer, sociologist, economist, political scientist and philosopher. He helped develop the field of microeconomics and the Pareto Principle was named after him.[341]

Vince Lombardi – (1913-1970) An American football coach, Vincent Thomas "Vince" Lombardi is best known as the head coach of the Green Bay Packers during the 1960s, when he led the team to three consecutive league championships and five in seven years, including winning the very first two Super Bowls. The National Football League's Super Bowl trophy is named in his honor.[342]

Virginia Woolf – (1882-1941) An English author, essayist, publisher, and short story writer, Adeline Virginia Woolf is regarded as one of the foremost modernist literary figures of the 20th century.[343]

W. Clement Stone – (1902-2002) An American-born businessman, philanthropist, and self-help author, W. Clement Stone went from rags to riches by following the principles he learned from Napoleon Hill's *Think and Grow Rich*. He also became an "angel" to others (e.g., he took an alcoholic, Og Mandino, and lifted him to great heights; Mandino became the publisher of *Success Magazine* at the time).[344]

W.C. Fields – (1880-1946) An American comedian, actor, juggler and writer, William Claude Dukenfield was known for his comic persona as a misanthropic and hard-drinking egotist.[345] The appearance of his large, bulbous nose (known as *rhinophyma* in the medical profession) is a common sign in alcoholics.

Warren Buffett – (born 1930) An American business magnate, investor, and philanthropist, Warren Edward Buffett is widely regarded as one of the most successful investors in the world. He is the primary shareholder, chairman and CEO of Berkshire Hathaway and is consistently ranked among the world's wealthiest people.[346]

William Foege, MD – (born 1936) An American-born physician, author, and epidemiologist, William Herbert Foege is credited with helping to eradicate smallpox. His book, *House on Fire: The Fight to Eradicate Smallpox* was published in 2011.[347]

William Shakespeare – (1564-1616) An English poet, playwright and actor, William Shakespeare is widely regarded as the greatest writer in the English language and the world's pre-eminent dramatist.[348] Years ago, my children and I had the great fortune of traveling to England with a group from the University of Texas-Pan American Theatre Department. One of the highlights of our trip was a tour of Shakespeare's birthplace and home in Stratford-upon-Avon!

Winston Churchill – (1874-1965) An English-born Conservative politician and statesman known for his leadership of the United Kingdom during World War II, Sir Winston Leonard Spencer-Churchill served as Prime Minister twice and is widely regarded as one of the greatest wartime leaders of the century.[349]

Woody Allen – (born 1935) An award-winning American screenwriter, director, actor, comedian, author, and playwright, he was born Allan Stewart Konigsberg. As a comic, he developed the persona of an insecure intellectual, which he says is quite different than his real-life personality.[350]

Zig Ziglar – (born 1926) An American best-selling author, salesman, and motivational speaker, Hilary Hinton "Zig" Ziglar emphasizes Christian values in his presentations. *See You at the Top* and *Success for Dummies* are among his many great books.[351] I met Zig about 20 years ago after one of his classic motivational presentations in Canada and I've been a fan ever since!

NOTES –

1. http://dictionary.reference.com/browse/dedication?s=t#wordorgtop

2. http://dictionary.reference.com/browse/dedicate

3. http://dictionary.reference.com/browse/acknowledge#wordorgtop

4. http://dictionary.reference.com/browse/foreword?s=t#wordorgtop

5. http://dictionary.reference.com/browse/foreword#wordorgtop

6. http://dictionary.reference.com/browse/preamble?s=t#wordorgtop

7. *Become a Better You: 7 Keys to Improving Your Life Every Day*, Joel Osteen, Simon & Schuster audio, 2007, Disc 2, Track 6.

8. Ibid.

9. Ibid.

10. Ibid, Track 7.

11. *Body Language – Explained,* Annie Finnigan, WomansDay.com, February 2, 2012.

12. Ibid.

13. "Indians Far From Bashful at Chow," *Los Angeles Times*, Art Rosenbaum, Los Angeles, Calif.: Oct 18, 1950. pC3 (1 page).

14. In the 2004 Olympic and Paralympic games, University of British Columbia psychology researcher Jessica Tracy found that winning poses are innate rather than learned. She found that athletes, both sighted and blind and across all cultures, tended to raise their arms, tilt their head up and puff out their chest. The expressions of defeat, which include slumped shoulders and a narrowed chest, were also found to be largely universal. Here is the study: "Olympic Athlete Study Shows That Pride and Shame are Universal and Innate Expressions," *Science Daily*, Jessica Tracy and David Matsumoto, August 11, 2008. http://www.sciencedaily.com/releases/2008/08/080811200018.htm

15. http://dictionary.reference.com/browse/alphabet?s=t#wordorgtop

16. http://dictionary.reference.com/browse/attitude?s=t

17. http://dictionary.reference.com/browse/aptitude?s=t#wordorgtop

18. **The Five Major Pieces to the Life Puzzle: A Guide to Personal Success**, Jim Rohn, Dickinson Press Inc, 1991, p32.

19. **Twelve Pillars**, Jim Rohn and Chris Widener, Jim Rohn International and Chris Widener International, 2010, p60.

20. Ibid.

21. **The Dictionary of Cliches**, James Rogers, Ballantine Books, 1985, p31.
    Birds of a feather flock together: This cliché refers to the fact that people who share similar interests and views tend to associate with one another. The phrase is based on the observation that birds in a group, whether flying or on the ground, are usually from the same species. The following dates back to 1545 England: "Byrdes of on kynde and color flok and flye all-wayes to gether." By 1680, John Bunyan's *The Life and Death of Mr. Badman* reflects the figurative phrase, "They were birds of a feather,... they were so well met for wickedness."

22. Please go to *www.TheCompoundEffect.com*, click on the "Free Resources" tab, and you will find an *Association Evaluator* worksheet that you can print. In the worksheet you will list the top five people you associate with, you will evaluate their level of success in nine different areas, and you will organize them into three categories: disassociations, limited associations, and expanded associations. In addition, you will list potential mentors who can accelerate your growth and even help you with accountability.

23. http://dictionary.reference.com/browse/believe?s=t

24. http://dictionary.reference.com/browse/believe?s=t#wordorgtop

25. http://www.keithvitali.com/

26. *Zig Ziglar's Spiritual Journey* CD, Get Motivated Seminars, Inc, 2003, Track 1.

27. Ibid.

28. http://dictionary.reference.com/browse/call?s=t

29. http://dictionary.reference.com/browse/me?s=t

30. *The Jim Rohn Sampler Audio CD*, Jim Rohn, 2002.

31. *Progress in Action* webinar, Michael Bernoff, http://www.ultimatelifecompany.com/speaker/1773/78

32. **The Brand Within: The Power of Branding from Birth to the Boardroom**, Daymond John with Daniel Paisner, Display of Power Publishing, 2010, p168.

33. http://dictionary.reference.com/browse/discipline?s=t

34. http://dictionary.reference.com/browse/disciple?s=t#wordorgtop

35. **Tae Kwon Do for Everyone,** José Luis Hinojosa, MD, Infinity Publishing, 2003, p186.

36. **Twelve Pillars**, Jim Rohn and Chris Widener, Jim Rohn International and Chris Widener International, 2010, p103.

37. Ibid.

38. *The Compound Effect - Audio Program*, Darren Hardy, SUCCESS Media, 2011.

39. **Twelve Pillars**, Jim Rohn and Chris Widener, Jim Rohn International and Chris Widener International, 2010, p54.

40. http://dictionary.reference.com/browse/education?s=t

41. **The Dictionary of Cliches**, James Rogers, Ballantine Books, 1985, p228.   *Out of the woods:* Clear of danger or difficulty. In England it is "out of the wood," which reflects the 1792 quote by Mme. D'Arblay (Frances Burney) from *Diary and Letters:* "Mr. Windham says we are not yet out of the wood, though we can see the path through it."

42. The Thrilla in Manila was the 3rd and final bout between Muhammad Ali and Joe Frazier. It took place in October 1, 1975 and was for the Heavyweight Championship of the World. Frazier did not come out for the 15th round, so Ali won by TKO. http://en.wikipedia.org/wiki/Thrilla_in_Manila

43. *SUCCESS* CD, SUCCESS Media, April 2010, John C. Maxwell, Track 5.

44. http://en.wikipedia.org/wiki/2005_World_Taekwondo_Championships

45. Stephen Cameron and James J. Heckman, "The Dynamics of Educational   Attainment for Black, Hispanic, and White Males," *Journal of Political Economy,* 109, June 3, 2001, p673-748.

46. **Goal: To Double the Rate of Hispanics Earning a Bachelor's Degree**, Georges Vernez and Lee Mizell, Santa Monica, Calif.: Rand Education, Center for Research on Immigration Policy, Jun 25, 2001, vii.

47. **Voices from the Nueva Frontera: Latino Immigration in Dalton, Georgia**, Donald Edward Davis, Thomas M. Deaton, David P. Boyle, University of Tennessee Press, Aug 15, 2009, p126.

48. *SUCCESS* CD, SUCCESS Media, November 2009, Jim Rohn, Track 5.

49. *SUCCESS* CD, SUCCESS Media, August 2010, Brian Tracy, Track 2.

50. **Success for Dummies**, Zig Ziglar, IDG Books Worldwide, Inc, 1998, p336.

51. http://dictionary.reference.com/browse/focus?s=t

52. http://dictionary.reference.com/browse/focus?s=t#wordorgtop

53. **How to Win Friends and Influence People**, Dale Carnegie, Simon and Schuster, 1936, p76.

54. Ibid, p75.

55. Why People 'Never Forget a Face,' December 8, 2006, http://www.physorg.com/news84812336.html

56. A rhythm in traditional verse, especially in Shakespeare, where a line has five groups of syllables characterized by an unstressed syllable followed by a stressed syllable (i.e., the accent is on the second

syllable). http://en.wikipedia.org/wiki/Iambic_pentameter

57. http://dictionary.reference.com/browse/give?s=t

58. http://dictionary.reference.com/browse/give?s=t#wordorgtop

59. *Coveted Wisdom: A Highly Effective Leader,* Stephen Covey, Success.com, December 2, 2008.

60. Scott Murray, "Making a Difference: Jim & Jill Kelly's Commitment to Hunter's Hope Helps Others," *Philanthropy World*, Vol 12, Issue 4, 2007, p27.

61. Ibid, p29.

62. Ibid.

63. *The Science of Good Deeds: The helper's high could help you live a longer, healthier life,* Jeanie Lerche Davis, Reviewed by Louise Chang, MD for WebMD, http://www.webmd.com/balance/features/science-good-deeds

64. Ibid.

65. Ibid.

66. http://dictionary.reference.com/browse/habit?s=t#wordorgtop

67. http://www.berkshirehathaway.com/2010ar.2010ar.pdf

68. Ibid.

69. http://dictionary.reference.com/browse/insult?s=t

70. http://dictionary.reference.com/browse/saltant?s=t

71. **The Wit and Wisdom of Abraham Lincoln: The Best Stories By & About America's Most Beloved President**, Anthony Gross (Editor), 2005.

72. **The Dictionary of Cliches**, James Rogers, Ballantine Books, 1985, p247.
Put up your dukes: The correlation between the word "dukes" and "fists" is vague. Perhaps it derives from the Latin *dux*, which means *leader;* one leads with one's fists. Apparently, *Macmillan's Magazine* from Great Britain, used the word (with a translation in parenthesis) in the following reference from 1879: "I said I would not go if he put his dukes (hands) on me."

73. **The Dictionary of Cliches**, James Rogers, Ballantine Books, 1985, p232. *Paper Tiger:* Something or someone not as tough or dangerous as first appeared. It seems the phrase was first coined by Chairman Mao from the People's Republic of China in 1946, when he referred to political ultraconservatives as "paper tigers."

74. **Tae Kwon Do for Everyone,** José Luis Hinojosa, MD, Infinity Publishing, 2003, p180.

75. **The Dictionary of Cliches**, James Rogers, Ballantine Books, 1985, p111. *Foam at the mouth:* To show anger; this is an analogy to a rabid dog, which behaves in an erratic or menacing fashion. By 1440, it was already applicable to humans, as in this line from *Jacob's Well*: "The man...fomyd out at his mowth."

76. http://www.lettersofnote.com/2012/01/to-next-burglar.html

77. **A Return To Love: Reflections on the Principles of A Course in Miracles**, Marianne Williamson, Harper Collins, 1992, p190-191.

78. http://dictionary.reference.com/browse/just?s=t

79. http://dictionary.reference.com/browse/right?s=t

80. *SUCCESS* CD, SUCCESS Media, March 2009, Roger Dawson, Track 4.

81. *The Compound Effect - Audio Program*, Darren Hardy, SUCCESS Media, 2011.

82. http://dictionary.reference.com/browse/kinetic

83. **Plan Your Work / Work Your Plan,** James R. Sherman, PhD, Crisp Publications, Inc, 1991.

84. http://dictionary.reference.com/browse/lead and http://dictionary.reference.com/browse/-ship

85. http://dictionary.reference.com/browse/lead?s=t#wordorgtop

86. Jim Rohn: How to Avoid Being Broke and Stupid, http://www.youtube.com/watch?v=_TjXy2pJXJI

87. Ibid.

88. *The Slight Edge: Secret to a Successful Life - Audio Book*, Jeff Olson, Momentum Media, 2006, Disc 3.

89. http://johnmaxwellonleadership.com/2010/10/03/the-five-levels-of-leadership-now-a-book/

90. Ibid.

91. *SUCCESS* CD, SUCCESS Media, October 2010, John C. Maxwell, Track 4.

92. http://dictionary.reference.com/browse/manner and http://dictionary.reference.com/browse/-ism

93. *SUCCESS* CD, SUCCESS Media, November 2009, Jim Rohn, Track 5.

94. *Body Language – Explained,* Annie Finnigan, WomansDay.com, February 2, 2012.

95. Ibid.

96. Ibid.

97. **Body Language: Easy Ways to Get the Most from Your Relationships, Work and Love Life**, Mark Asher, Carlton Books Limited, 1999, p28.

98. *What do dilated pupils mean?,* Libby Pelham, Body Language Expert, Dec 17, 2010. http://www.bodylanguageexpert.co.uk/what-do-dilated-pupils-mean.html

99. **Body Language: Easy Ways to Get the Most from Your Relationships, Work and Love Life**, Mark Asher, Carlton Books Limited, 1999, p48.

100. **Tae Kwon Do for Everyone,** José Luis Hinojosa, MD, Infinity Publishing, 2003, p43.

101. **Body Language: Easy Ways to Get the Most from Your Relationships, Work and Love Life**, Mark Asher, Carlton Books Limited, 1999, p81.

102. **The Tonic,** José Luis Hinojosa, MD, SterlingHouse Publisher, 2001, p42.

103. **Success for Dummies**, Zig Ziglar, IDG Books Worldwide, Inc, 1998, p37.

104. *Does it take fewer muscles to smile than it does to frown?*, Cecil Adams, January 16, 2004. http://www.straightdope.com/columns/read/2489/does-it-take-fewer-muscles-to-smile-than-it-does-to-frown

105. http://www.sun-angel.com/quotes/view_author.php?AID=97&QA=Rabbi%20Samson%20Raphael%20Hirsch

106. http://dictionary.reference.com/browse/net and http://dictionary.reference.com/browse/work

107. Memorable quotes from *Six Degrees of Separation,* 1993. Accessed from IMDB.com - http://www.imdb.com/title/tt0108149/quotes

108. **Outliers: The Story of Success**, Malcolm Gladwell, Little, Brown and Company, 2008, p19.

109. Ibid, p123.

110. http://dictionary.reference.com/browse/option?s=t#wordorgtop

111. *SUCCESS* CD, SUCCESS Media, July 2011, John C. Maxwell, Track 4.

112. "Doctor Says Kissing Can Kill," *McAllen Monitor*, Jim McKone, Gotta Have Arts/Festiva Section, McAllen, Texas, Dec 28, 2001.

113. **The Testament,** John Grisham, Island Books, 1999, p296-297.

114. http://dictionary.reference.com/browse/patience?s=t#wordorgtop

115. http://dictionary.reference.com/browse/passion?s=t#wordorgtop

116. Ibid.

117. *SUCCESS* CD, SUCCESS Media, November 2009, Jim Rohn, Track 5.

118. **The Teacher's Manual,** Thomas H. Palmer, 1840, Boston, p221-223.

119. http://en.wikipedia.org/wiki/Thomas_Edison

120. Ibid.

121. http://www.rjgeib.com/thoughts/friend/lincoln-failures.html

122. *SUCCESS magazine*, Publisher's Letter (Darren Hardy), August 2009.

123. "Walk On," ESPN, E:60, April 14, 2012.

124. http://munchanka.blogspot.com/2011/07/animation-letters-project.html

125. *The Secret Law of Attraction* Audio CD program, Napoleon Hill, Read by Michael McConnohie, Highroads Media, Inc, 2008, Disc 3, Track 2.

126. http://dictionary.reference.com/browse/quest?s=t#wordorgtop

127. **Peak Performance Principles for High Achievers**, John R. Noe, Berkley Books, 1984, p55.

128. Ibid.

129. Ibid.

130. *The Slight Edge: Secret to a Successful Life - Audio Book*, Jeff Olson, Momentum Media, 2006, Disc 3.

131. http://dictionary.reference.com/browse/responsible#wordorgtop

132. http://dictionary.reference.com/browse/responsible?s=t#wordorgtop

133. http://dictionary.reference.com/browse/respond#wordorgtop

134. **Outliers: The Story of Success**, Malcolm Gladwell, Little, Brown and Company, 2008, p194.

135. Ibid, p195.

136. **The Last Lecture**, Randy Pausch with Jeffrey Zaslow, Hyperion, 2008, p175.

137. Ibid.

138. **Tae Kwon Do for Everyone,** José Luis Hinojosa, MD, Infinity Publishing, 2003, vii.

139. **The Last Lecture,** Randy Pausch with Jeffrey Zaslow, Hyperion, 2008, p176.

140. *The Compound Effect - Audio Program,* Darren Hardy, SUCCESS Media, 2011.

141. http://dictionary.reference.com/browse/sales?s=t#wordorgtop

142. http://dictionary.reference.com/browse/sell?s=t#wordorgtop

143. *SUCCESS* CD, SUCCESS Media, October 2010, Tom Hopkins, Track 3.

144. Ibid.

145. Ibid.

146. *SUCCESS* CD, SUCCESS Media, September 2009, Paul Zane Pilzer, Track 3.

147. *Shark Tank,* ABC Network, January 27, 2012.

148. *The Sales Training Series: Sell Yourself Before You Sell Your Company,* http://www.cantonscore.org/the-sales-training-series-sell-yourself-before-you-sell-your-company.htm

149. *Sell Me This Pencil – Focus on Customer Needs, Not Your Product's Features,* Russ Lombardo, http://www.bizymoms.com/business/Article/Sell-Me-This-Pencil---Focus-on-customer-needs--not-your-product-s-features/27

150. **Master and Disciple,** José Luis Hinojosa, MD, Cafepress.com, 2006, p124.

151. http://dictionary.reference.com/browse/team?s=t#wordorgtop

152. **Success for Dummies**, Zig Ziglar, IDG Books Worldwide, Inc, 1998, p3.

153. Ibid, p4.

154. Ibid.

155. Ibid.

156. Ibid.

157. Ibid, p5.

158. **Wooden: A lifetime of Observations and Reflections On and Off the Court,** Coach John Wooden with Steve Jamison, McGraw-Hill, 1997, p113.

159. **The Dictionary of Cliches**, James Rogers, Ballantine Books, 1985, p209. *Their (or My) name is Legion:* There are many in the group; I am part of a large group. In the Roman army, a legion consisted of nearly 6,000 soldiers and "legion" came to mean a great number of individuals with a common purpose – a team, if you will. Also, the Bible includes a passage (Mark 5:9) where Jesus is speaking with a man of blemished spirit and asks his name. The reply is, "My name is Legion: for we are many."

160. *SUCCESS* CD, SUCCESS Media, October 2010, Jim Rohn, Track 5.

161. http://dictionary.reference.com/browse/universal?s=t#wordorgtop

162. http://dictionary.reference.com/browse/universe?s=t#wordorgtop

163. http://dictionary.reference.com/browse/law?s=t#wordorgtop

164. http://en.wikipedia.org/wiki/Vilfredo_Pareto

165. Rooney, Paula (October 3, 2002), *Microsoft's CEO: 80–20 Rule Applies To Bugs, Not Just Features*, ChannelWeb, http://www.crn.com/news/security/18821726/microsofts-ceo-80-20-rule-applies-to-bugs-not-just-features.htm

166. "Apple Inc: The Greatest Turnaround in Corporate History?," *Oxygen: The Turnaround Magazine*, Issue 6, Autumn 11.

167. Nick Bilton, "Apple Is the Most Valuable Company", *New York Times*, 9 August 2011

168. United Nations Development Program (1992), *1992 Human Development Report*, New York: Oxford University Press.

169. http://www.ahrq.gov/research/ria19/expriach1.htm

170. http://www.politifact.com/oregon/statements/2012/feb/23/alan-bates/does-20-percent-population-really-use-80-health-ca/

171. **The HELP Secret: Hi Energy Leadership Pointers**, José Luis Hinojosa, MD, CafePress.com, 2009, p15-16.

172. http://www.lifehack.org/articles/productivity/how-to-use-parkinsons-law-to-your-advantage.html

173. *The Slight Edge: Secret to a Successful Life - Audio Book*, Jeff Olson, Momentum Media, 2006, Disc 3.

174. **Rosi Milagros**, José Luis Hinojosa, MD, CafePress.com, 2008.

175. **Outliers: The Story of Success**, Malcolm Gladwell, Little, Brown and Company, 2008, p40.

176. Ibid.

177. http://dictionary.reference.com/browse/value?s=t#wordorgtop

178. http://dictionary.reference.com/browse/valiant?s=t#wordorgtop

179. **Report Card on Rape: Medical and Self-Defense Strategies for Obtaining Straight A's,** José Luis Hinojosa, MD, Vantage Press, 1990, p26.

180. http://www.lyrics007.com/The%20Beatles%20Lyrics/Help!%20Lyrics.html

181. http://dictionary.reference.com/browse/will?s=t#wordorgtop

182. **Lou Ferrigno: Lou Ferrigno's Guide to Personal Power, Bodybuilding, and Fitness for Everyone**, Lou Ferrigno, 1994, p55.

183. Ibid, p56.

184. Ibid, p26.

185. Memorable quotes from *Stand and Deliver*, 1988. Accessed from IMDB.com - http://www.imdb.com/title/tt0094027/quotes

186. Memorable quotes from *Enter the Dragon*, 1973. Accessed from IMDB.com - http://www.imdb.com/title/tt0070034/quotes

187. http://dictionary.reference.com/browse/excuse?s=t#wordorgtop

188. http://dictionary.reference.com/browse/cause?s=t#wordorgtop

189. *SUCCESS* CD, SUCCESS Media, October 2009, Jim Rohn, Track 5.

190. Ibid.

191. Ibid.

192. **The Dictionary of Cliches**, James Rogers, Ballantine Books, 1985, p111. *Fool's gold:* Something that isn't what it appears to be; an illusion; perhaps a trick? Iron pyrites were found in coal seams and were frequently mistaken for gold because they have a golden or brassy appearance. In 1576, explorer Martin Frobisher returned to England with what he thought was "gold mineral." It wasn't gold; it was pyrite. In 1882, the *Boston Journal of Chemistry* picked up the name "fool's gold" to refer to iron pyrite.

193. *Shark Tank*, ABC Network, Feb 10, 2012.

194. http://dictionary.reference.com/browse/yo-yo?s=t#wordorgtop

195. **Magnets for Health: A Practical Guide,** José Luis Hinojosa, MD, Kroshka Books, 2000, p24.

196. Ibid.

197. http://en.wikipedia.org/wiki/Meditation_XVII

198. Ibid.

199. http://dictionary.reference.com/browse/enthusiasm?s=t

200. **Peak Performance Principles for High Achievers,** John R. Noe, Berkley Books, 1984, p467.

201. http://dictionary.reference.com/browse/passion?s=t

202. http://dictionary.reference.com/browse/zest?s=t

203. **Peak Performance Principles for High Achievers,** John R. Noe, Berkley Books, 1984, p111.

204. **Success for Dummies,** Zig Ziglar, IDG Books Worldwide, Inc, 1998, p16.

205. http://jobs.aol.com/articles/2012/01/25/the-power-of-recognition-in-the-workplace-infographic/

206. Globoforce Workforce Mood Tracker, The September 2011 Report, *The Impact of Recognition on Employee Retention,* Globoforce Ltd, 2011. WorkforceMoodTracker_September2011_ONLINE.pdf

207. http://jobs.aol.com/articles/2012/01/25/the-power-of-recognition-in-the-workplace-infographic/

208. *SUCCESS* CD, SUCCESS Media, March 2011, Daniel Pink, Track 3.

209. **The HELP Secret: Hi Energy Leadership Pointers**, José Luis Hinojosa, MD, CafePress.com, 2009, p5.

210. Ibid.

211. http://www.freedomwritersfoundation.org/site/c.kqIXL2PFJtH/b.4104711/k.8887/Request_the_Freedom_Writers/apps/ka/ct/contactus.asp?c=kqIXL2PFJtH&b=4104711&en=fgLGLPMxFeKILPPvH5IEJWMAKiKRJYOBI8IOJoMEIqK3H

212. **Success for Dummies**, Zig Ziglar, IDG Books Worldwide, Inc, 1998, p56.

213. Ibid, p55-56.

214. Ibid, p55.

215. http://dictionary.reference.com/browse/epilogue?s=t#wordorgtop

216. "To Read or Not to Read: A Question of National Consequence," National Endowment for the Arts, November 2007, Table 3-I, p45. www.nea.gov/research/toread.pdf

217. *SUCCESS magazine*, Publisher's Letter (Darren Hardy), May 2011, p6.

218. I incorporated this type of "active" reading in 1976, mainly because of necessity. All the markings I was filling my books' pages with were for survival. It's reassuring and validating to hear experts such as Harvey Mackay (*SUCCESS* CD, November 2009, Track 3) recommend the same approach to reading – actually, to "studying." Great minds think alike!

219. Refer to Chapter 5 – Education, Part II, where Brian Tracy recommends to read an hour per day, which equals one book per week, which means you will successfully read 50 books in a year! This will put you so far ahead of the competition.

220. *SUCCESS* CD, SUCCESS Media, November 2009, Joel and Victoria Osteen, Track 2.

221. "To Read or Not to Read: A Question of National Consequence, National Endowment for the Arts," November 2007, Table 3-I, p95. www.nea.gov/research/toread.pdf

222. http://dictionary.reference.com/browse/win#wordorgtop

223. http://en.wikipedia.org/wiki/Abdelkader_El_Djezairi

224. http://en.wikipedia.org/wiki/Sufi

225. http://en.wikipedia.org/wiki/Abraham_Lincoln

226. http://www.leg.state.or.us/bates/ and http://en.wikipedia.org/wiki/Alan_Bates_(politician)

227. http://einstein.biz/biography

228. http://en.wikipedia.org/wiki/Albert_Mehrabian

229. http://www.valleycentral.com/sports/story.aspx?id=556501

230. http://en.wikipedia.org/wiki/Aristotle

231. http://pixar.wikia.com/Austin_Madison

232. http://en.wikipedia.org/wiki/The_Beatles

233. http://www.imdb.com/title/tt0145487/

234. http://en.wikipedia.org/wiki/Benjamin_Franklin

235. http://en.wikipedia.org/wiki/Brian_Tracy

236. *SUCCESS* CD, SUCCESS Media, August 2010, Brian Tracy, Track 2.

237. http://en.wikipedia.org/wiki/Bruce_Lee

238. http://www.imdb.com/title/tt0094715/quotes

239. http://en.wikipedia.org/wiki/Charles_M._Schwab and http://en.wikipedia.org/wiki/Charles_R._Schwab

240. http://www.chriswidener.com/speaking and www.madeforsuccess.com/

241. http://en.wikipedia.org/wiki/C._Northcote_Parkinson

242. http://en.wikipedia.org/wiki/Dale_Carnegie

243. http://en.wikipedia.org/wiki/Daniel_Levitin

244. http://www.danielpaisner.com/

245. http://en.wikipedia.org/wiki/Daniel_H._Pink

246. http://darrenhardy.success.com/about/

247. http://en.wikipedia.org/wiki/David_Brinkley

248. http://www.uchospitals.edu/physicians/david-song.html

249. http://en.wikipedia.org/wiki/Daymond_John

250. http://en.wikipedia.org/wiki/Diana_L%C3%B3pez

251. https://portal.utpa.edu/utpa_main/daa_home/coah_home/theatre_home/theatre_facultystaff/Dr.%20Jack%20Stanley

252. http://en.wikipedia.org/wiki/Earl_Nightingale

253. http://en.wikipedia.org/wiki/Edward_Burgess_Butler

254. http://archive.org/stream/edwardbbutler18500chic#page/20/mode/2up

255. http://en.wikipedia.org/wiki/Edward_James_Olmos

256. http://en.wikipedia.org/wiki/Eleanor_Roosevelt

257. http://en.wikipedia.org/wiki/Epictetus

258. http://en.wikipedia.org/wiki/Erin_Gruwell

259. http://www.findagrave.com/cgi-bin/fg.cgi?page=gr&GRid=19881251

260. http://www.amazon.com/Erwin-O-Smigel/e/B001HD1EZ4/ref=ntt_athr_dp_pel_1

261. http://www.sc.edu/fitzgerald/biography.html

262. http://en.wikipedia.org/wiki/Harvey_Mackay

263. http://www2.talbot.edu/ce20/educators/view.cfm?n=henry_cope

264. http://en.wikipedia.org/wiki/Henry_Ford

265. http://en.wikipedia.org/wiki/Henry_Russell_Sanders

266. http://sports.espn.go.com/nfl/news/story?id=2125887

267. http://en.wikipedia.org/wiki/Isabel_Gauthier

268. http://jackiechan.com/biography

269. http://en.wikipedia.org/wiki/Jaime_Escalante

270. http://en.wikipedia.org/wiki/Jawaharlal_Nehru

271. http://lopeztaekwondo.net/instructors/master-jean-lopez/

272. http://www.slightedge.org/pages/about-jeff

273. http://en.wikipedia.org/wiki/Jeffrey_Zaslow

274. *The Compound Effect - Audio Program*, Darren Hardy, SUCCESS Media, 2011.

275. http://www.ucomparehealthcare.com/drs/jesus_rodriguez/

276. http://www.jillk.org/

277. http://en.wikipedia.org/wiki/Jim_Kelly

278. http://en.wikipedia.org/wiki/Jim_Rohn

279. http://www.jimwagnertraining.com/aboutjimwagner.html

280. http://en.wikipedia.org/wiki/Joe_Friday

281. http://en.wikipedia.org/wiki/Joe_Navarro

282. http://en.wikipedia.org/wiki/Joel_Osteen

283. http://en.wikipedia.org/wiki/Johann_Kaspar_Lavater and http://en.wikipedia.org/wiki/Physiognomy

284. http://en.wikipedia.org/wiki/John_Bunyan

285. http://en.wikipedia.org/wiki/John_C._Maxwell

286. http://en.wikipedia.org/wiki/John_D._Rockefeller

287. http://en.wikipedia.org/wiki/John_Donne

288. http://en.wikipedia.org/wiki/John_F._Kennedy

289. http://en.wikipedia.org/wiki/John_Grisham

290. http://en.wikipedia.org/wiki/John_Guare

291. http://en.wikipedia.org/wiki/John_Wooden

292. http://en.wikipedia.org/wiki/Jos%C3%A9_Jes%C3%BAs_M%C3%A1rquez

293. http://human-factors.arc.nasa.gov/organization/personnel_view.php?personnel_id=59

294. http://en.wikipedia.org/wiki/Julius_Caesar

295. http://en.wikipedia.org/wiki/Keith_Vitali

296. http://www.temple.edu/psychology/curby/index.htm

297. http://en.wikipedia.org/wiki/Laozi

298. http://lesbrown.org/lesbrown.com//lesbrown.com/english/meet_lesbrown.html

299. http://en.wikipedia.org/wiki/Earl_of_Chesterfield

300. http://en.wikipedia.org/wiki/Lori_Greiner

301. http://en.wikipedia.org/wiki/Lou_Ferrigno

302. http://en.wikipedia.org/wiki/Malcolm_Gladwell

303. https://portal.utpa.edu/utpa_main/daa_home/coah_home/theatre_home/theatre_facultystaff/Marian%20Monta

304. http://en.wikipedia.org/wiki/Marianne_Williamson

305. http://en.wikipedia.org/wiki/Mark_Cuban

306. http://en.wikipedia.org/wiki/Mark_L%C3%B3pez_(taekwondo)

307. http://en.wikipedia.org/wiki/Mark_Twain

308. http://en.wikipedia.org/wiki/Martin_Luther_King,_Jr.

309. http://www.amazon.com/Never-Lick-A-Frozen-Flagpole/dp/1416533397/ref=sr_1_6?s=books&ie=UTF8&qid=1334083906&sr=1-6#reader_1416533397

310. http://www.michaelbernoff.com/About

311. http://en.wikipedia.org/wiki/Michael_Jordan

312. http://en.wikipedia.org/wiki/Muhammad_Ali

313. http://en.wikipedia.org/wiki/Napoleon_Hill

314. http://en.wikipedia.org/wiki/Napoleon_III

315. http://en.wikipedia.org/wiki/Neil_Armstrong

316. http://www.quotesl.com/nelson_boswell/

317. http://en.wikipedia.org/wiki/Oprah_Winfrey

318. http://en.wikipedia.org/wiki/Pablo_Picasso

319. http://en.wikipedia.org/wiki/Paul_Zane_Pilzer

320. http://www.teambardatsos.com/documents/34.html

321. http://en.wikipedia.org/wiki/Peter_Jackson

322. http://www.presleyswagerty.com/presley.html

323. http://en.wikipedia.org/wiki/Ralph_Waldo_Emerson

324. http://en.wikipedia.org/wiki/Randy_Pausch

325. http://en.wikipedia.org/wiki/Robert_Herjavec

326. http://en.wikipedia.org/wiki/Samson_Raphael_Hirsch

327. http://en.wikipedia.org/wiki/Robert_Kiyosaki

328. http://www.mindperk.com/DawsonBio.htm

329. http://www.ronwhitetraining.com/about-ron-white-memory-expert

330. http://en.wikipedia.org/wiki/Stephen_Covey

331. http://en.wikipedia.org/wiki/Stephen_G._Post

332. http://en.wikipedia.org/wiki/Steve_jobs

333. http://en.wikipedia.org/wiki/Steven_L%C3%B3pez

334. http://en.wikipedia.org/wiki/Thomas_Edison

335. http://www.goines.net/Writing/if_at_first_you.html

336. http://en.wikipedia.org/wiki/Thomas_%C3%A0_Kempis

337. http://www.mindperk.com/HopkinsBio.htm

338. http://www.freedomwritersfoundation.org/atf/cf/%7Bb2a26556-086e-4ffa-af6c-dc4ee722c801%7D/BIO-MAURICIO-TONY.PDF

339. http://en.wikipedia.org/wiki/Tony_Robbins

340. http://www.lcc.gatech.edu/~fischer/

341. http://en.wikipedia.org/wiki/Vilfredo_Pareto

342. http://en.wikipedia.org/wiki/Vince_Lombardi

343. http://en.wikipedia.org/wiki/Virginia_Woolf

344. http://en.wikipedia.org/wiki/W._Clement_Stone

345. http://en.wikipedia.org/wiki/W._C._Fields

346. http://en.wikipedia.org/wiki/Warren_Buffett

347. http://en.wikipedia.org/wiki/William_Foege

348. http://en.wikipedia.org/wiki/William_Shakespeare

349. http://en.wikipedia.org/wiki/Winston_Churchill

350. http://en.wikipedia.org/wiki/Woody_Allen

351. http://en.wikipedia.org/wiki/Zig_Ziglar

Photos –

July 8, 2006 - Grand Champion© was officially "unveiled" at the Universal Martial Arts Hall of Fame USA Expo and 10th Anniversary Banquet & Induction Ceremonies in Houston, TX. Thanks to Grand Champion©, I was inducted as Martial Arts Entrepreneur of the Year.

As Official Doctor of the US National TaeKwonDo Team at the 1995 World Championships in Manila. Peter Bardatsos (*far left*) and Jean Lopez (*2nd from left*) are referenced in *The Language of Winners!*

(*L-R*) Dad, me, Eric Lee, Mom, and my sister, May. Mom was in the final stages of her battle against the Big C.

Reflections of an Old Man is always a crowd pleaser!

My latest Trading Card features an old man & his cane.

(*L-R*) My pride & joy – Laura, Alexis, and JL. It was Alexis' 2011 graduation from high school.

I won the Gold Medal at the 2006 National TKD Championships in Knoxville, Tennessee.

With Zig Ziglar in Ontario, Canada after one of his great Motivational Presentations. Zig is one of the best!

At poolside with Presley Swagerty at his home in Texas. He's the #1 Money Earner in his Direct Sales company.

With Chuck Norris in Hollywood (1998).

As a photographer, I enjoy creating inspirational posters.

The first time I met my good friend, Keith Vitali, was in Pasadena, CA (1993).

Close up of my 2005 World Championship ring from my win in Rosenheim, Germany and the card game it inspired, Grand Champion©.

Playing Luis Rivera in *Tales of the Hidalgo Pumphouse*. Thunderstorms and The Headless Man can give you insomnia!

With José Ardón, the #1 Hispanic Money Earner in the Direct Sales Industry worldwide. He's wearing his Millionaire ring and I'm wearing my World Champion ring.

Yet another reason why
Personal Improvement books are so important!

(*L-R*) My wife, Maria Elena, with nieces and business leaders Gladys Rodriguez and Leoni Olivares (a new author). Leoni is a Domestic Violence spokesperson and she provided great publishing advice for *The Language of Winners!*
Thanks, Leoni!

Celebrating success with my lovely wife, Maria Elena.

About the Author –

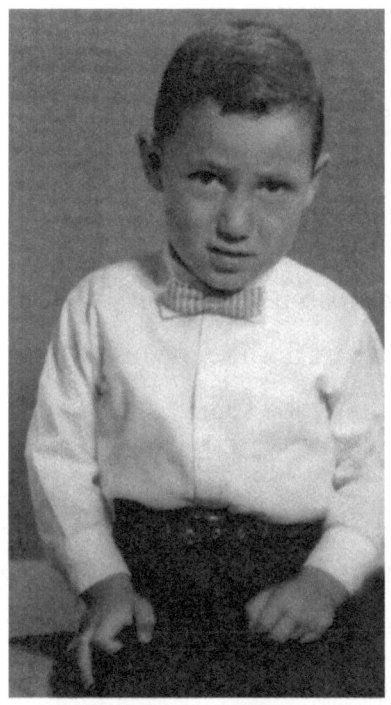

Even as a child,
I'd dress for success!

One of my passions is
playing my saxophone.

February 24, 1958, Monday, 10:15 pm, Nuevo Laredo, Tamaulipas, México.

INDEED, IT WAS A COLD, WINTER EVENING and the unborn child did not know what time it was; he just wanted to be born; he had some things to do and places to go; there was a journey he needed to embark upon. And so it was that José Luis "Jay-el" Hinojosa came to this world, blessing the lives of Homero Hinojosa Guerra and Rosalinda Fernández Ramón and becoming the second of their six children. The proud parents named him after a famous bullfighter that the mother wanted to honor. All day and all night, there had been fireworks and a celebration – and the baby thought it was for him, but it turns out February 24th is Mexican Flag Day, a national holiday. Still, to this day, Jay-el believes that the day he was born an entire nation celebrated his arrival.

The delivery room was not a sterile hospital room either – on the contrary, it was a tiny home with dirt floors. The bed where he was born is still around and it will belong to him in the near future. Surely, anyone who survives that kind of a birth environment is a fighter, a winner. And fight is what he has had to do most of his life. In actuality, anyone who achieves some level of success has had to overcome multiple obstacles in the process, and Jay-el is no exception.

At the age of 7 years, Jay-el's family immigrated to the United States. Throughout his elementary school years, he was the frequent victim of bullying, mainly from one huge, mean kid who was not discriminatory – he bullied everyone. One day in the 5th grade, the bully was making his rounds and it was again Jay-el's turn to be bullied. It was then that he had an epiphany

– he decided to strike first! Jay-el punched the bully in the gut and knocked the wind out of him. With a smile, the much smaller Jay-el looked up at the towering giant with the cyanotic (blue) face, admiring what he had just accomplished. When the bully regained his breath, he proceeded to punish Jay-el like never before – and that would be the last of it, for he never again bullied him. So, whenever it was his turn for another beating, the bully would simply skip him. It was a very empowering and liberating feeling for Jay-el!

In high school, Jay-el played clarinet, alto saxophone, and flute for several professional "Tejano" bands while also playing in the school band. He graduated from Eagle Pass High School in south Texas in 1976 and went to Brown University for his undergraduate studies. There, he discovered the martial arts and quickly advanced through the ranks, receiving his very first black belt on December 3, 1978 in New York City, under the tutelage of Grand Master Duk Sung Son. Jay-el Hinojosa received a Bachelor's Degree in Biology from Brown and then enrolled at the University of Cincinnati College of Medicine for his medical studies. Still practicing martial arts, Jay-el achieved his MD on June 6, 1985 and went back to Texas to complete his Residency Training in Family Medicine in McAllen, Texas. After a successful 25-year Family Practice and almost 1,000 deliveries as part of the Obstetric component to his practice, Dr. Jay-el officially retired in January 2010. Always striving to be the best, Dr. Jay-el Hinojosa's medical accolades were many, culminating in 2009 when he was named one of *America's Top Family Doctors* by Consumers' Research Council of America in Washington, DC. He was also a world-renowned Sports Medicine physician, having traveled all over the globe as the Official Doctor for the United States National Tae Kwon Do Team in the 1990s.

Dr. Hinojosa has been a martial arts leader and teacher for more than 34 years and has won many titles, including *World Championships* in Germany and México, multiple Hall of Fame awards, including a *Lifetime Achievement Award*, and he is a crowd favorite with his powerful, creative, and highly entertaining routines – most notably, his award winning form entitled *Reflections of an Old Man*, where he dresses up as an elderly man with a cane and dazzles the crowd while reminiscing about his youth. Speaking of youth, Dr. Hinojosa has three children (JL, Laura, and Alexis) who always inspire him; he is also happily married to Maria Elena Hinojosa.

As an innovator, Dr. Hinojosa invented the popular game *Grand Champion®*, the first ever card game related to the martial arts. *The Language of Winners!* marks the ninth book he has authored – please look at the beginning of *The Language of Winners!* for a listing of his other books.

He is a playwright (*Rosi Milagros* – a two act play that takes place in 1924 México) and co-wrote the screenplay for an independent feature length film (*Campeón: A Journey of the*

Heart). His book *Master and Disciple,* like *Grand Champion®,* teaches good moral values and won the 2008 Universal Martial Arts Hall of Fame *Author of the Year* award for Dr. Hinojosa.

Dr. Hinojosa is equally fluent in Spanish as he is in English keynote presentations. He is a stage actor and has also appeared in several feature-length films. His most recent acting work was in the world premiere run (Nov. 2011 and Jan. 2012 in three south Texas cities) of *Tales of the Hidalgo Pump House,* where he played one of the lead characters, Luis Rivera, and had the opportunity to display his singing, dancing, and comedic timing; in his most recent film, he played the villain in the feature-length 2009 Warrior Pictures film *Campeón: A Journey of the Heart.*

As a professional speaker, Dr. Hinojosa shares his experiences with his audiences with such passion and clarity, that he always "connects." It is no wonder that Dr. Jay-el Hinojosa is highly sought out as a motivational and inspirational speaker not only in the USA, but also in México. He is a specialist in *Leadership and Success* topics, with his most popular keynotes being: *The Making of a Leader, Dream Your Way to Success, The Five Business Lessons to Learn from Breaking Boards,* and *Develop a World Champion Attitude.*

To Order Additional Copies of

The Language of Winners!

By
World Champion
José Luis Hinojosa, MD

see quantity discounts below:

(Retail: $22.95)

1-9 Books $22.95 each

10-24 Books $19.95 each

25+ Books $17.95 each *(and Free Shipping!)*

Go to **www.TheLanguageOfWinners.com** or write to us at:

> The Language of Winners!
> PO Box 3550
> Edinburg, Texas, USA 78540

- • -   - • -   - • -

For those of you who yearn to become the Master Achiever that you are meant to be, we invite you to book Dr. Hinojosa as a ***Motivational Speaker*** at your next corporate event and start to... Unleash Your Potential!

Simply go to **www.TheMasterAchiever.com**

My winning notes:

www.ingramcontent.com/pod-product-compliance
Lightning Source LLC
Chambersburg PA
CBHW030134170426
43199CB00008B/62